INSPIRING STORIES FOR CHILDREN

Saints of India

Bal-Mukund Character Building Series

Bal-Mukund Coordinator: Aruna Kannan
Editorial Team: Shreya Bhat, Anand Rao
Portraits: Sanjay Sarkar
Design: Graphics Spot
Acknowledgement: Jaishree Srinivasan, Sandeep Sethi,
                           Madhu Gupta

Published by:
Jagadguru Kripalu Yog
7405 Stoney Point Drive
Plano, TX 75025
USA
www.jkyog.org

ISBN 978-0-9826675-6-9

Printed by:

Elegant Prints
www.elegant-prints.com

Dedication

The Bal-Mukund Character Building Series is dedicated to our Beloved Spiritual Master, Jagadguru Shree Kripaluji Maharaj, who is illuminating this world with the purest rays of Divine knowledge and love.

He has taught us by his example, the importance of nurturing children with love and care, to help them realize a glorious future. He has given us the supreme process of building a noble value system into impressionable young minds by teaching them selfless Divine love.

We pray that by his blessings this series will be helpful in inspiring, elevating and molding the children of today, who in turn will create a better world for tomorrow.

Jagadguru Shree Kripaluji Maharaj

पवित्र जीवन एवं महान व्यक्तित्व की नींव की प्राप्ति के हेतु बाल्यावस्था में ही दिये गये संस्कारों से पड़ती है। अतएव माता पिता द्वारा बच्चों को सर्वश्रेष्ठ प्रेमोपहार यही होता है कि उन्हें बचपन से ही दैवी गुण संपन्न बनाया जाय।

उन दैवी गुणों का प्राकट्य परमात्मा की निष्काम भक्ति द्वारा अंतःकरण की शुद्धि से ही होता है।

अतः आध्यात्मिक शिक्षा द्वारा बच्चों के मन में भगवद्भक्ति का संचार करना उनके उज्ज्वल भविष्य के हेतु सर्वाधिक कल्याणकारी है।

भक्त प्रह्लाद ने कहा था -

कौमार आचरेत् प्राज्ञो धर्मान् भागवतानिह (भागवत ७/६)

अर्थात् बाल्यावस्था से ही भागवत धर्म का अनुसरण प्रारंभ कर देना चाहिये।

प्रस्तुत मुकुंद चरित्र निर्माण पुस्तक माला भारतीय संस्कृति एवं शास्त्रों, वेदों पर आधारित एवं सही कल्याण कारी आध्यात्मिक-शिक्षा युक्त है। मेरी यही कामना है कि बालवृंद इससे अवश्य लाभान्वित होंगे।

अथ्वदीय -

जगद्गुरु कृपालु महाराज

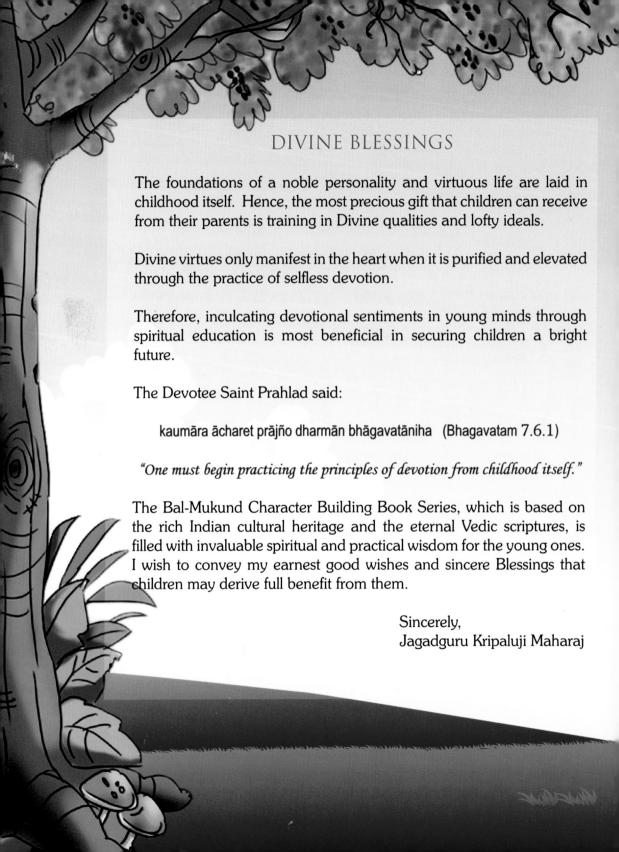

DIVINE BLESSINGS

The foundations of a noble personality and virtuous life are laid in childhood itself. Hence, the most precious gift that children can receive from their parents is training in Divine qualities and lofty ideals.

Divine virtues only manifest in the heart when it is purified and elevated through the practice of selfless devotion.

Therefore, inculcating devotional sentiments in young minds through spiritual education is most beneficial in securing children a bright future.

The Devotee Saint Prahlad said:

kaumāra ācharet prājño dharmān bhāgavatāniha   (Bhagavatam 7.6.1)

"One must begin practicing the principles of devotion from childhood itself."

The Bal-Mukund Character Building Book Series, which is based on the rich Indian cultural heritage and the eternal Vedic scriptures, is filled with invaluable spiritual and practical wisdom for the young ones. I wish to convey my earnest good wishes and sincere Blessings that children may derive full benefit from them.

Sincerely,
Jagadguru Kripaluji Maharaj

About
Bal-Mukund
Playground for Vedic Wisdom

Bal-Mukund is a specially designed personality development program for children, envisioned by Swami Mukundananda. It endeavors to:

❖ Educate young minds in the knowledge of Vedic wisdom to lead a virtuous life.

❖ Enthuse the spirit of giving with a service attitude.

❖ Encourage problem solving with courage, confidence and faith.

❖ Entertain creativity, expand power of concentration and focus.

❖ Elevate young minds to higher consciousness and fill their hearts with love and reverence for God.

The Bal-Mukund program is designed for the holistic development of a young one's physical, intellectual, social and spiritual faculties. Activities include Yoga, Pranayam, Meditation for children, Shlokas, Kirtans, Stories/discussion, Games, Language classes, Arts and Crafts.

For Bal-Mukund program details and centers:
www.bal-mukund.org

INTRODUCTION TO THE BAL-MUKUND CHARACTER BUILDING SERIES

The mark of a civilized society is the loving care it takes of its children. They are not merely children; they will soon be other people's husbands and wives, and parents of grandchildren. They possess God's life force that is yearning to make them Presidents, Scientists, Engineers, Doctors, Artists, Writers, and Musicians. Just as the acorn carries the potential of becoming an oak tree, children carry in them infinite potential for future greatness. Caring parents and teachers see this potential, and carefully cultivate and nurture it.

Parents and teachers are partners of God. They are working with the Creator of the Universe in shaping human nature and forging the future world. Each day they make deposits in the memory banks of their children. These deposits must be uplifting, and ennobling to their impressionable minds, which are sponge-like and very sensitive to the impressions they receive from their mentors. Children possess a remarkable amount of passion to go after their ideals. They throw themselves completely, heart and soul, into everything. The impressions they receive in these formative years mould their vision for the future. Loving parents and teachers teach their children to dream with their eyes open, of a noble and fulfilling life. They fill their hearts with lofty ideals and inspiring thoughts, and then fondly watch as their wards strive to attain the goals that have been mapped in them in their childhood.

Jagadguru Shree Kripaluji Maharaj teaches that best inheritance we can leave for children is good training in character building. A strong and sound value system built into them will remain until death. It will be the foundation for a successful and rewarding life. Hence, the values we inspire them to cherish are of paramount importance.

Children must be taught that money and luxurious possessions alone will not give happiness, but a virtuous life will be a continual feast.

Time spent in inculcating such values in children is an investment into the future. It is the finest gift of love from parents to their children. The Bal-Mukund Character Building Series contains invaluable instructions, famous verses, bhajans, stories, life histories and information about festivals, for building values in children. For ease of remembrance, the values that are required for triumph in life have been grouped with the letters of the acronym "KRIPALU". These set of values will teach children to be heroic from within, and instill nobleness in their thought, word and deed.

The compendium of stories, biographies, festivals, sayings, kirtans and prayers in this series of books has been chosen from the Vedic scriptures and the rich literary heritage of India. They convey powerful messages to educate, encourage, enthuse, and entertain young minds. Most importantly, they fill the heart with love and reverence for God, which is the essence of all morality. We hope they will be cherished by teachers, parents and children alike, who will meditate upon them, learn them and make them a part of their lives.

Swami Mukundananda

The "KRIPALU" Values

 for Kindness

Helping nature, Service attitude, Caring for others, Compassionate to the sufferings of others, Non-violence towards all beings, Forgiveness, and Seeing the Divinity in others.

for Respect

Respect for Elders, Respect for Teachers, Respect for Authority, Respect for each other, Courtesy, Good Manners, Not seeing faults in others, Being non-judgmental, Acceptance of the differing viewpoints of others, Obedience to Elders and Authority

for Integrity

Truthfulness, Purity of thoughts and intentions, Self-discipline and control over mind and senses, Restraint from temptation, Restraint from harmful influences like drugs, cigarettes, and alcohol, restraint from gambling, Associating with good people and giving up association of those who are a bad influence.

for Perseverance

Hardworking, Enduring, Patient, Dedication to the work at hand, Tenacity to bear difficulties and not give up, Overcoming obstacles through persistence, Keeping a positive "I can do it" attitude, Single-mindedness towards goal, Using tact and intelligence and mental power to solve a problem.

for Accountability

Taking full responsibility for ones deeds, Taking the onus for mistakes, Responsibility for correcting them, not blaming others or having a whining nature, Taking responsibility for organizing oneself and one's work, Accepting the law of karma that what happens to us is a result of our own actions, Being punctual to our time commitments.

for Love for God

Trust in God, Faith in His protection, Acceptance of His will, Keeping a positive attitude in every situation with Faith in His Grace, A Sense of Gratitude for all that God has given us, Belief that He is with us and watching us always, Doing all actions for His pleasure, unconditional devotion to Him.

for Unassuming

Modesty, Unpretentiousness, Simplicity, Humility, Not boasting or showing off, Reverence for the Greatness of God, Faith that everything belongs to God and not to us, Realizing that God has a grand scheme why things happen and we all have a tiny role to play in His design.

Contents

|| VALMIKI ||

Maharishi Valmiki is considered as the father of Indian poetry. He is revered as the Adi Kavi, or the poet of poets of the Sanskrit language. He composed the shloka that set the base and defined the form of Sanskrit language. He is famous as the author of the Ramayan, consisting of 24,000 verses.

EARLY YEARS

Valmiki was born to sage Prachetasa, and was called Ratnakar in his childhood. One day, while in the forest, young Ratnakar got lost and was adopted by a hunter. Under the love and care of his foster parents, Ratnakar forgot his own parents. With his foster father's guidance, Ratnakar trained to be an excellent hunter himself. He was married to a beautiful girl from a hunter's family. As his family got large, he found it impossible to feed them. As a result, he took to robbery and began looting people passing from one village to another.

TURNING POINT

One day, he happened to attack the great sage Narad who was passing through the jungle. Narad was playing on his Veena and singing praises of the Lord. This began a transformation in Ratnakar. Sage Narad questioned him why he was committing so many sins. He replied that it was for the maintenance of his family. Narad then asked him whether his family would share in the fruits of his sins. Ratnakar replied that he had no doubt they would. Narad told him to go and get this confirmed from his family. When Ratnakar asked his family the same question, he was dismayed to discover that none of them was willing to share the fruits of his sins. This incident taught him about the selfish nature of everyone in the world.

Ratnakar went back to sage Narad and asked how he could attain God. Sage Narad asked him to chant the name "Ram." Ratnakar was unable to bring the Divine Name of the Lord to his lips, because of the heavy burden of his sins. Narad then asked him to utter "Ma Ra" repeatedly, until he returned. Ratnakar obeyed the instructions of his Guru completely, and sat in one spot, continuously chanting "Ma Ra, Ma Ra" for years. He was so deeply absorbed in his chanting that in course of time his body was covered by anthill. The Sage Narad finally returned, removed the anthill, and bestowed his grace on him. Ratnakar began to be called Valmiki, or the one who was covered by an anthill. Narad also gave him the title of Brahmarshi, or God-realized Saint. Valmiki then established his ashram on the banks of the Ganga.

HIS WORKS

Legend says that once Valmiki was going to the River Ganga with his disciple, for a bath. On the way, they came across the Tamasa stream. Valmiki looked at the clear water of the stream, and compared it to the mind of a good man. As he was saying so, he saw two birds flying overhead. He was relishing the joyous chirps of the bird couple, when one of the birds was hit by a hunter's arrow and it fell down dead. The

plight of the poor birds made Valmiki sad and angry at the same time. It was at this moment that he uttered a Sanskrit verse.

mā niṣāda pratiṣṭhāṁ tvamagamaḥ śāśvatīḥ samāḥ

yat krauñcamithunādekam avadhīḥ kāmamohitam

The verse means, "You will find no rest for the rest of eternity, since you have killed this unsuspecting bird couple, while they were absorbed in love." To his surprise, the verse was in lyrical and metered language. Brahma then gave him a vision, and asked him to write the Ramayan.

Valmiki then wrote the entire Ramayan, in the same poetic meter. The amazing thing was that he wrote it before the actual descension of Lord Ram. By virtue of his Divine vision, he was able to foresee the leelas that Shree Ram would do during his descension on the earth. In addition, Valmiki also wrote the Yoga Vasishtha.

LATER DAYS

Valmiki made his ashram in the forest, and continued to reside there, awaiting the descension of Shree Ram to take place. During His avatar kaal (descension period), Lord Ram, Lakshman and Seeta came to Valmiki's ashram. Valmiki received Ram, Lakshman, and Seeta with the utmost devotion. This meeting was described later by Tulsidas in his Hindi Ramayan. Later, Lord Ram's children, Luv and Kush, became Valmiki's first disciples to whom he imparted the wisdom of the Ramayan.

|| GAUTAM BUDDHA ||

Gautam Buddha was the founder of Buddhism, one of the major religions of the world. He was an avatar (descension) of the Supreme Lord, Shree Vishnu. Buddha, or the Enlightened One was born and raised in a royal family but attained true knowledge, which he later spread to the world through the tenets of his teachings.

EARLY YEARS

Siddharth Gautam was born in late sixth century B.C., in the village Lumbini, which is a part of modern day Nepal. His father, King Suddhodana was the leader of the Shakya clan. His mother, Queen Maya, died soon after his birth. In his early childhood, it was prophesied that Siddharth would grow up to be a world conqueror, but if he was exposed to the miseries of the world, he would become a spiritual teacher. Siddharth's father preferred that he grow up to become a warrior, and so he shielded his son from the realities of the world. The young prince lived a life of great luxury, unaware of the pain and poverty outside his palace, until the age of twenty-nine.

TURNING POINT

One day, to fulfil his curiosity about life outside the palace walls, young Siddharth asked his charioteer to take him around the countryside. There, he saw an old man suffering in pain. He was disturbed to know that people eventually grow old. Then he saw a sick person and a dead corpse. These encounters saddened him greatly, and left a deep impression on his mind. He realized that all living beings without exception have to experience the sufferings of birth, sickness, old age and death. Having led a sheltered life until then, he was shaken up by these harsh realities.

Siddharth also happened to see an ascetic and was surprised to see how calm he looked. Siddharth was told that the ascetic had renounced the world and was free from the fear of suffering and death. After his return to the palace, Siddharth was very disturbed and restless. He got news that his wife Yashodhara had given birth to his son, but his mind did not seem to experience any happiness. He wanted to realize the true meaning of life, and in that quest, he shaved off his head, wore the robes of a sadhu and left the palace at night in secrecy.

Even though Siddharth learned philosophy and meditation from many teachers, he still sought answers to many questions. He performed many severe austerities in the company of ascetics, to attain enlightenment. When intense penance and pain did not help him, Siddharth realized that he needed to follow a middle path between pleasure and pain. When he decided to sacrifice the path of penance, his companions assumed that he had given up his quest and abandoned him. Undeterred, Siddharth reached Bodh Gaya (presently in Bihar in North India) and sat for meditation under a peepal (fig) tree, that later came to be known as the Bodhi tree. It was under this tree that Siddharth attained enlightenment in his war

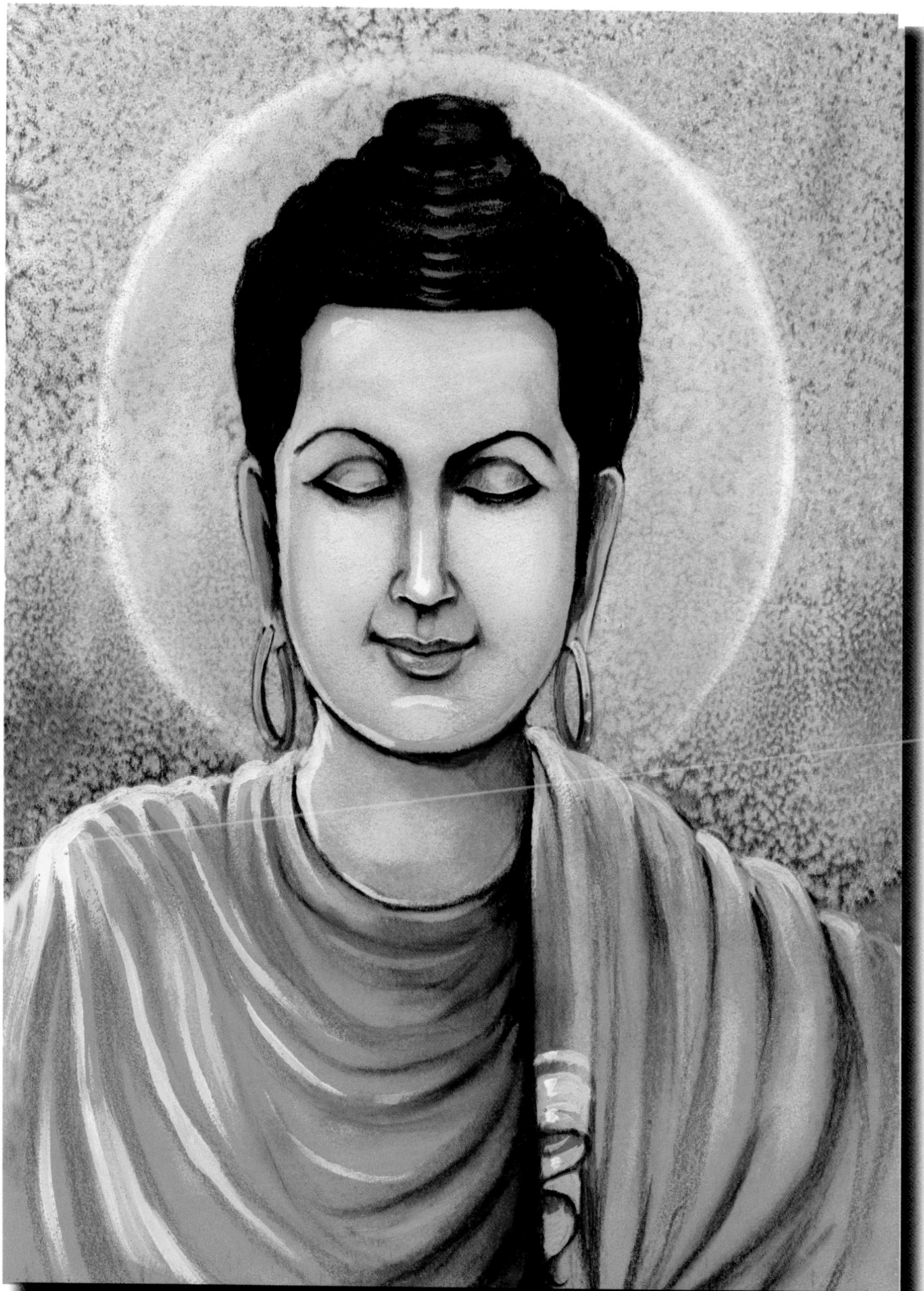

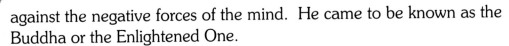

against the negative forces of the mind. He came to be known as the Buddha or the Enlightened One.

HIS TEACHINGS

After attaining enlightenment, the Buddha was not very keen on teaching, as he was aware that what he had learned could not be communicated through words. It had to be experienced through discipline of the mind. However, he was moved by compassion to do something for humanity. He travelled in search of his five companions, to what is now Uttar Pradesh in Northern India. Having found them, he preached the first sermon to them based on the four noble truths. These four truths are:

1. There is suffering in life

2. The cause of suffering is attachment

3. Suffering can be finished

4. The eight-fold path is the way to get release from suffering

The eight-fold path consists of: right view, right intention, right speech, right action, right livelihood, right effort, right mindfulness and right concentration. As progress is attained through this path over several lifetimes, a person can achieve salvation or liberation from the cycle of suffering and death.

The teachings of Buddha have inspired several schools of philosophy and practices. In Tibet, the Dalai and Panchem Lama followers have their own tradition based on the tenets of Buddhism first taught by Gautam Buddha. In China and Japan, Zen Buddhism involves a meditative adaptation of the teachings. In Sri Lanka, Theravada Buddhism combines primitive belief in spirits with traditional teachings of the Buddha.

MAHA SAMADHI

The Buddha widely preached the knowledge that he had received through enlightenment. At the age of 80, he suddenly announced that he would soon be leaving his earthly body. Gautam Buddha left this world, having spread his teachings across India and neighboring countries.

‖ MAHAVIR ‖

The name Mahavir means 'Great Hero'. Although Jainism existed before Mahavir was born, he is accredited with popularizing it throughout India. He was the twenty-fourth Tirthankar, which means a holy Jain teacher. As a religious reformer, he revised the Jain teachings, thus establishing the central tenets of Jainism.

EARLY YEARS

Mahavir was born in 599 B.C. in the ancient kingdom of Lachuar in the State of Bihar in North India. His father, Siddharth, was a King and a great astrologer. His mother, Queen Trishala, had very beautiful dreams about Mahavir, even before he was born. In her dreams, she saw signs telling her that her son would be a great soul and guide the world to be free from miseries.

Mahavir's arrival was very lucky to his father's kingdom, which saw great growth and prosperity from the time he appeared in his mother's womb. Mahavir's first name was Vardhamana, which means "ever growing". He was later also known as "Sanmati".

Even as a young prince, Mahavir was very virtuous. He used to constantly meditate and reflect on life. He learned the arts of music and literature. When Mahavir was very young, King Siddharth arranged for a teacher to instruct him in weapons. The teacher soon found out that his student knew more than what he could teach him.

Mahavir's bravery impressed everyone. One day, a celestial god named Sangama, transformed himself into a large snake and came to frighten Mahavir. Instead of getting scared, Mahavir showed his compassion and took the snake in his hand in order to protect it from the others and let it go in the fields. He was not scared at all. While some believe that he got the name Mahavir (Great Hero) after this incident, there are many others who believe he was called Mahavir because he conquered himself, which is a far more difficult thing.

TURNING POINT

Mahavir lived a royal life as a prince of Bihar. He married Yashoda and had a daughter named Riyadarshana. By the time Mahavir turned thirty, he saw through his powers that he had many lives in the past. He started reflecting on the nature of soul and its purpose. He realized that all worldly things were temporary and that the soul was separate from the body. The soul was bonded due to the laws of karma, and the soul could only be freed when one got rid of karma. He realized that being born as a human was a great blessing, because it allowed him to meditate on the nature of the soul.

He was convinced that he had to leave home in order to progress spiritually. His mother tried to dissuade him, but he told her that it was impossible to get happiness in the material world, because it was the abode of disease, sorrow, pain and death.

PENANCE

He gave up all his worldly possessions and went to the forest, as a monk. He fasted for several days and constantly reflected on the nature of the soul. He kept moving from one place to another. Most of his meditation was done in standing posture.

He spent twelve years doing intense meditation. At the end of these twelve years, he became enlightened. It is believed that the celestial gods wanted him to reveal to others what he had acquired. However, they realized that because he had not spoken for twelve years, he could not communicate easily in the people's language. Hence, the Gods sent Gautama, a learned brahmin, to interpret for him. As soon as Mahavir saw Gautama, words began coming from his mouth and Gautama started translating them. Gautama became one of Mahavir's earliest disciples.

HIS TEACHINGS

For the next thirty years, Mahavir traveled across the country preaching the eternal truths of spiritual knowledge. He traveled barefoot and without clothes, even in very cold climates. People from all over would come to listen to him. He preached that every individual seeks temporary pleasure from material possessions, which result further in greed, anger, hatred and other vices. According to him, every soul is in bondage to karma. To free oneself from karma, Mahavir taught the importance of right faith, right knowledge and right conduct. He preached that to follow right conduct, one must take the five vows – to cause no harm to any living being, to speak the truth always, to not steal from anyone, to indulge in no sensual pleasure and to detach from all material possessions.

Mahavir considered non-violence to be the highest virtue of humans. He said that all living beings desire to live. Hence, no one should take to killing. His concept of non-violence was not limited to killing, but to anything that caused pain to others, be it a rude behavior or harsh words. All such actions that hurt others were to be shunned.

FINAL DAYS

At the age of 72, on Deepavali day, Mahavir attained Nirvana (Salvation) in a town called Pawapuri. Jains celebrate Deepavali as the day prophet Mahavir attained liberation or Moksha. Sculpted images of him in the state of Nirvana can be found all over India.

|| JAGADGURU SHANKARACHARYA ||

Shankaracharya was a great philosopher who propagated the philosophy of Advaita vada, or non-dualism. It states that the world is a transient reality and the Brahman (self) is the ultimate reality. Several schools of Hinduism follow the path of Advaita philosophy (non-dualism) taught by Shankaracharya. Shankaracharya is considered by many to be an avatar of Lord Shiv Himself. He was the first Hindu saint in modern history to be honored with the title of Jagadaguru.

EARLY YEARS

He was born to a devout brahmin couple in the village of Kaladi in Kerala. His parents prayed to Lord Shiv for a son, and so when the child was born, he was aptly named Shankara.

Even at an early age, Shankara's brilliance and extraordinary spiritual powers were obvious to all. After his thread ceremony, as was the custom, Shankara would visit people's houses to collect bhiksha (alms) for his meal. One day, he went to a poor woman's home, who could only offer him some dried amla (gooseberries). Moved by her poor plight, Shankara chanted the Kanaka Dhara Stotra and much to the amazement of the poor woman, there was a shower of gold coins.

While Shankara was a little child, his father passed away, leaving his mother to take care of him. Once when his mother was ill, Shankara made the Purna River change its path, so that his mother would not have to travel a great distance for her bath. Right from childhood, Shankara wanted to renounce the world and become a sanyasi, but his mother would not let him go. One day, while he was bathing in the river, a crocodile caught hold of his leg. On hearing his screams, Shankara's mother came rushing to the scene. Shankara said, "Mother! My death is now certain. Please allow me to fulfil my desire by taking sanyas before the crocodile eats me." Left with no choice, his mother immediately agreed, and Shankara mentally accepted the renounced order of sanyas. To his mother's surprise, the crocodile released his leg. She was thankful to see her son alive and she gave her blessings to him on his spiritual journey. However, she made him promise that he would return to her at the time of her death.

When Shankara got the news that his mother was on her deathbed, true to his promise, he returned to meet her. During her last days, Shree Shankara instructed his mother to practice devotion to Lord Krishna. After her death, he fulfilled his duties by lighting her funeral pyre, even though he was forbidden to do so, as a sanyasi.

MEETING WITH THE GURU

On the banks of the river Narmada, Shankara met Acharya Govindapada, who recognized the brilliance of the young man and made him his disciple. Shankara learned the Vedic scriptures from his Spiritual Master and wrote several commentaries on them.

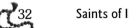

Although fated to live only till the age of sixteen, sage Ved Vyas himself appeared before Shankara and granted him another sixteen years of life to continue his work. Shankara moved to Kashi and continued writing commentaries on major Hindu scriptures. He wrote the famous bhajan, Bhajo Govindam, while at Kashi. The essence of this bhajan states that life is short-lived, like a dewdrop on a lotus petal that can fall anytime. Therefore, it is important to realize one's spiritual goals before giving up this physical body.

Once, in Kashi, a chandal blocked Shankara's way, and as the path was narrow, Shankara asked the chandal to move out of the way. The chandal in turn asked that Shankara preached Advaita - the oneness of everything with Brahman. Then why was he seeing the chandal as different from himself. Realizing that this was no ordinary being, Shankara fell at the feet of the chandal, who turned out to be Lord Shiv himself.

GRACE OF THE GURU

Many legendary anecdotes are narrated about Shankara and his disciples. His disciple, Sanandana, was drying the clothes of his Guru and suddenly Shree Shankara called him to the other bank of the river. Sanandana, little realizing that he would drown, started walking on the river. To everyone surprise, a lotus appeared at every step that he walked, and he crossed over to the other side unharmed! The grace of his Guru ensured that he would not drown. After this incident, the disciple came to be known as Padmapada .

POPULAR DEBATES

Shree Shankara travelled throughout India, and engaged in many great debates with leaders of different schools of thought. He went to all the prominent seats of learning, and defeated the scholars with his explanations. Consequently, he became known as "Jagadguru," or "Spiritual Master of the world."

One famous debate of Shankaracharya was with a renowned scholar Mandan Mishra. They debated for fifteen days, with Mandan Mishra's wife, Ubhaya Bharati acting as referee. Mandana Mishra accepted defeat but Ubhaya Bharati challenged Shankara to debate with her to complete the victory. At one point, to answer a question by Ubhaya Bharati on family life, Shankara left his own body and entered that of a dying king. Equipped with knowledge gained in the king's body, he was able to win the debate. According to the rules of the debate, Mandan Mishra became a sanyasi disciple of Shree Shankara. He was named Sureshwaracharya. His wife too became a Shankara's disciple.

HIS WORKS

Shankara wrote Bhashyas or commentaries on the Brahma Sutras, the Upanishads and the Gita. The Bhashya on the Brahma Sutras is called Shareerik Bhasya. Shankara wrote commentaries on Sanat Sujatiya and Sahasranama Adhyaya. His commentaries on logic and metaphysics are very widely acclaimed. His other important works include the Viveka Chudamani, Atma Bodha, Aparoksha Anubhuti, Ananda Lahari, Atma-Anatma Vivek, Drik-Drishya Vivek and Upadesh Sahasri. Shree Shankara wrote innumerable original works in verses, which are matchless in sweetness, melody and thought.

HIS TEACHINGS

Shankaracharya was born at a time when Buddhism had spread all over India. His task was to refute the Buddhist philosophy and re-establish the glory of the Vedas. During his early preaching life, Shree Shankara preached non-dualistic philosophy. He upheld the view that the soul is not different from the Supreme Brahman. He propounded that the Supreme Being is Nirgun (without the Gunas), Nirvishesh (without attributes), Nirakar (formless), and Akarta (non-agent). He is above all needs and desires. Preaching thus, he brought back the Buddhists into the fold of the Vedas.

During the last decade of his life, Shree Shankara accepted the dual nature of God. He accepted that the Supreme Lord is also Sagun (with all the Gunas), Savishesh (with all the attributes) and Saakar (with all forms). He composed innumerable verses in praise of Lord Krishna, Lord Ram, Lord Shiv and Mother Durga. His works includes some of the best poems in Indian literature, describing the beauty of Shree Krishna.

LAST DAYS

At the age of 32, Shankaracharya visited Kedarnath with his disciples where he expressed his wish to give up his material body. He delegated the responsibility of carrying forth his work to his four main disciples who were made heads of four institutions at Sringeri, Jagannath Puri, Dwaraka and Badrinath. He also gave the essence of all his teachings in ten verses. It is said that as the verses were being chanted, Shankaracharya went into samadhi and his body disappeared without a trace.

|| JAGADGURU NIMBARKACHARYA ||

Nimbarkacharya was a great saint and philosopher. He was a proponent of the Dvaitadvaita school of Hindu philosophy. He is believed to have been the avatar of the Sudarshan Chakra of Lord Shree Krishna.

His philosophy is counted amongst the six main schools of Vedant:

1. Advaita of Jagadguru Shankaracharya

2. Visisthadvaita of Jagadguru Ramanujacharya

3. Dwaita of Jagadguru Madhvacharya

4. Achintya Bhedabheda of Chaitanya Mahaprabhu

5. Shuddhadvaita of Vallabhacharya

6. Dvaitadvaita of Jagadguru Nimbarkacharya

Hindu scholars honor Nimbarkacharya as one of the four original Jagadgurus of the past.

EARLY YEARS

Nimbarkacharya was born to Aruna Muni, a great ascetic and his wife, Jayanti Devi who lived on the banks of Godavari in modern day Andhra Pradesh. According to the Nimbarka Sampradaya, his appearance day was in the year 3096 B.C. The date of his birth is subject to much controversy, as some historians state that he was born in the eleventh century. According to the Bhavishya Purana, the brahmins prayed to Lord Vishnu to protect them from the asuras. The Sudarshana Chakra of the Lord descended in the form of Nimbarkacharya, who was named Niyamananda at birth.

Niyamananda was a very bright child and became a scholar at a very young age. The legend goes that when Niyamananda was in his teens, Brahma, the Creator, visited his father's ashram in the guise of a sanyasi. As Niyamananda's father was away and there was no food in the house, his mother was at a loss over what to serve the guest. As sunset neared, she worried that they may have to suffer for violating the Atithi Dharm (rule of conduct towards guests), which instructs one to treat a guest as God. She knew that sanyasis do not partake of any meals after sunset. Niyamananda asked his mother not to worry and left with the promise that the sun would not set until after he had come back and served the guest. He went to the forest after placing the Sudarshan Chakra on a neem tree at the ashram, where it shone brightly like the sun. He then gathered fruits from the forest and served the guest. He removed the Sudarshan Chakra from the neem tree, after Brahma had eaten, and right away, it became pitch dark. Brahma was pleased with Niyamananda's devotion and named him "Nimbarka" (Nim means neem tree and Arka means the sun). He thus came to be called Nimbarkacharya. He was the embodiment of divine qualities such as love, kindness and mercy.

In search of a true Guru, he performed austere penance. Sage Narad was pleased with his penance, and blessed him with the knowledge of

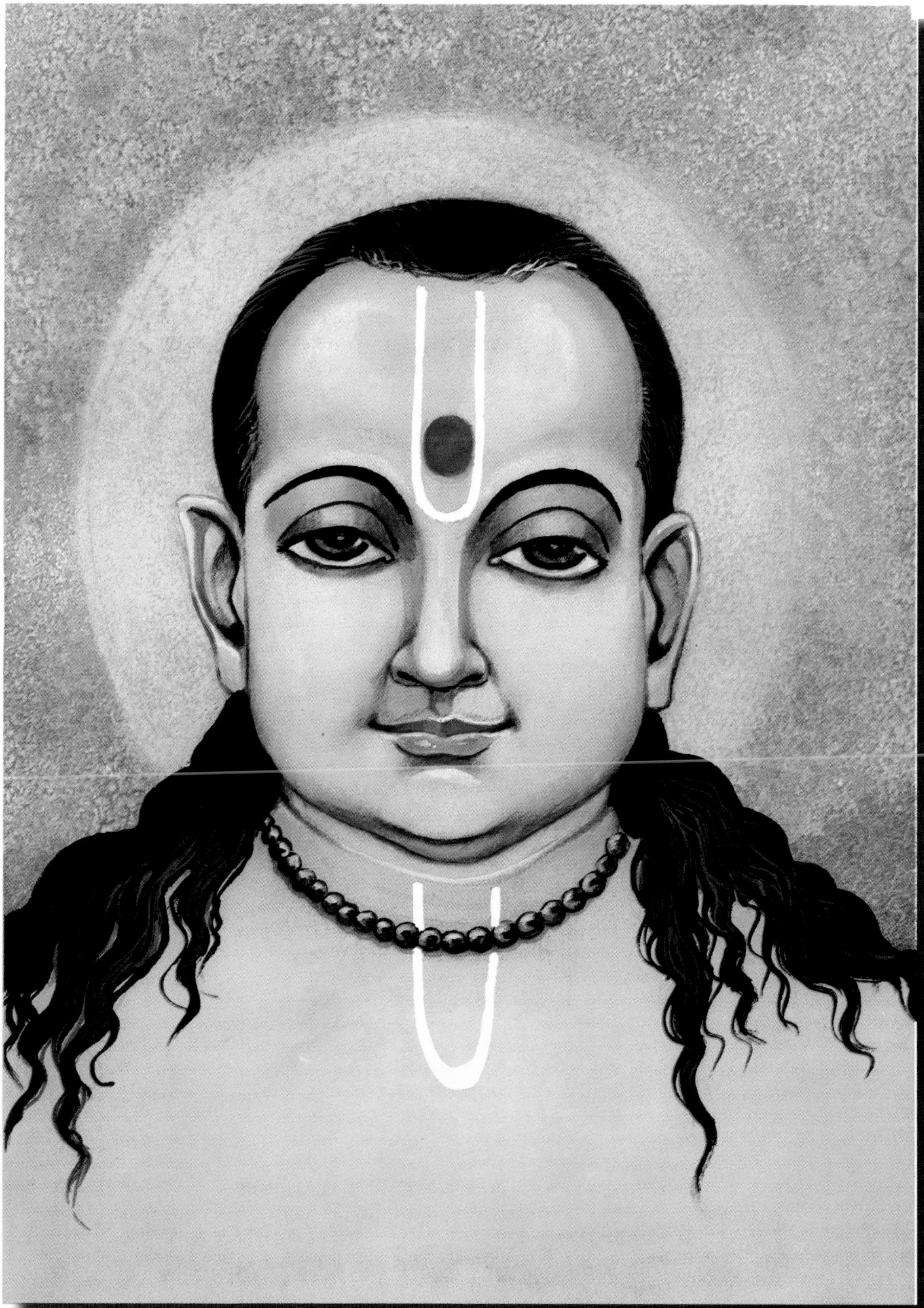

Vedanta. Niyamananda then meditated on Shree Radha Krishna, who instructed him to preach the path of *bhakti*.

HIS PHILOSOPHY

Nimbarkacharya propagated the Dvaitadvaita philosophy, which explains the existence of duality and non-duality at the same time. He stated that there are three entities: Bhagavan (God), Jeev (soul) and Maya (material energy). Jeev and Maya are both separate from Bhagavan, and yet part of Him. Both have attributes that make them different from Bhagavan but in some ways similar to Him. Thus, there are three real and eternal realities.

Nimbarkacharya laid down five aspects to the path of salvation: Karma (action), Vidya (knowledge), Upasana or Dhyana (meditation of the Lord), Prapatti (devotion and surrender to the Lord) and Gurupasatti (surrender to the Guru).

Nimbarkacharya spread the message of worshipping Shree Radha Krishna. Therefore, his followers hold the holy places related to Their pastimes in great reverence, such as Vrindavan, Nandgaon, Barsana and Govardhan. Even today, devotees visit the Shree Nimbarka temple in Neembgram, situated near Govardhan.

HIS WORKS

Nimbarkacharya wrote a bhashya (commentary) of the Brahma Sutra based on his philosophy, called the Vedant Parijat Sourabh. He authored many other literary works such as the Prata Smarana Stotram, Sadachar Prakash, Vedanta Kama Dhenu, Savisesh Nirvisesh Sri Krishna Stavam, Mantra Rahasya Shodashi, Radha Ashtak, etc. The greatest contribution of Nimbarkacharya's commentary on the Brahma Sutra appears to pre-date all the other commentaries on it, as there is no reference to the others in Nimbarkacharya's work. It thus seems that Nimbarkacharya belonged to an earlier era than the five other schools of Vedant.

|| JAGADGURU RAMANUJACHARYA ||

Ramanujacharya was a great philosopher and preacher of Shree Vaishnavism. He was born in the early twelfth century in the village of Shree Perumbudur, in modern day Tamil Nadu. Seeing his unfathomable knowledge of the Vedic scriptures, Ramanujacharya was acclaimed as Jagadguru, or Spiritual Master of the world. He was the third Jagadguru in Indian history, after Adi-Shankaracharya and Nimbarkacharya.

EARLY YEARS

His childhood name was Ilaya Perumal. Early in life, he lost his father, and was raised by his mother. He got married as a teenager, and shortly thereafter, his family moved to Kancheepuram. There, he studied Vedant under Yadav Prakash, a teacher of the Advaita philosophy. Many of Yadav Prakash's interpretations of the Vedas did not satisfy Ramanuja, and he would point out the mistakes to his Guru. This made Yadav Prakash jealous of Ramanuja and he plotted to have him killed. Fortunately, Ramanuja was able to escape, as his cousin,

who was also a student of Yadav Prakash, tipped him off.

Ramanuja then became a student under Kanchipurna, who was an acharya (teacher) of the Vishishtadvaita school of Vedic philosophy, which was gaining popularity at that time. Kanchipurna was a disciple of a great Vaishnav teacher, Yamunacharya. Ramanuja desired to meet the aged philosopher, Yamunacharya. However, just before he could reach him at Srirangam, Yamuncharya passed away. When Ramanuja came, he found that three fingers of the great Saint's dead body were curled. Ramanuja understood that Yamunacharya had three last wishes:

1. Teach the doctrine of Sharanagati (surrender) to God.

2. Write a bhashya, or commentary, on the Brahma Sutras of Ved Vyas, in accordance with the philosophy of Vishistadvaita.

3. Strengthen memories of the Saints Ved Vyas and Parashar.

Ramanuja resolved that he would fulfil these wishes. As Ramanuja vowed thrice to fulfil each of Yamunacharya's wishes, his fingers straightened one-by-one.

Ramanuja then learned Yamunacharya's philosophy from his disciple Mahapurna. Mahapurna was of lower caste, and Ramanuja's wife would serve him his meal and take a bath afterwards. This greatly annoyed Ramanuja, as he did not believe in these meaningless caste-based rituals. He entered the order of sanyas, and took the name of "Ramanuja Muni." Since he was like the king amongst sanyasis, he also came to be known as "Yati Raja."

He was invited to take over as the head of the Shrirangam Math. Before taking that position, he was given a mantra in his ear by an acharya named Nambi. The guru asked him not to divulge the mantra to anyone. Ramanujacharya disagreed with the instruction. He said that if the mantra was beneficial, there was no reason to keep it secret. He went to the crossroads and loudly announced it to the public. Thus,

Ramanujacharya mocked the tradition of receiving secret mantras from gurus in the ear.

HIS TEACHINGS

Ramanujacharya propagated the philosophy of Vishishtadvaita or qualified non-dualism. According to this school, God possess a form and attributes, that are all Divine and beyond Maya. Lord Narayan is the Supreme Lord of the universe, and the jeev (soul) is a servant of God. The goal of the soul is to surrender to God.

HIS WORKS

Ramanujacharya wrote a commentary on the Brahma sutras called the Shree Bhashya. It is one of the most scholarly commentaries on the scriptures ever written. Ramanuja's other works include the Vedant Saar (essence of Vedant), Vedant Sangraha (a resume of Vedant) and Vedant Deep (the light of Vedant).

LAST YEARS

Ramanuja preached the philosophy of devotion to Lord Vishnu far and wide. He visited all the sacred places in India including Kashi, Kashmir and Badrinath. Ramanuja travelled extensively in South India and helped to cleanse temples there of the unnecessary rituals that had crept into practice. He standardized the worship in these temples. He visited the Tirupathi hills, and endorsed the worship of Shree Vishnu in the temple there. He built several temples in the city of Mysore, and established it as the centre of his school of Vedant. As desired by his followers, he built a temple at Srirangam and installed his own image for worship. His physical body is preserved to this day in the sanctum sanctorum at the temple.

Ramanujacharya continued his ceaseless service towards spread of his philosophy until the age of 120 years, when he entered maha samadhi.

|| JAGADGURU MADHVACHARYA ||

Madhvacharya was a great religious reformer and philosopher of the thirteenth century A.D. He was the proponent of Dwaitavada (dualistic) school of bhakti philosophy. Madhvacharya is highly respected by Hindu scholars as the fourth Jagadguru in history, and is credited with upholding the essence of Bhakti in the medieval times. He is considered by many to be the third avatar of the celestial god Vayu, after Hanuman and Bheem.

EARLY YEARS

Acharya Madhva was born in the late twelfth or early thirteenth century in the South Indian temple town of Udipi, on the auspicious day of Vijaya Dashami. There is some debate on his exact year of birth. He was named Vasudev at birth, but was called Poornapragnya and Madhva in his later years. As a child, Vasudev had a great physique and was nicknamed Bheem. He astounded everyone with his remarkable

ability to grasp the most difficult topics of philosophy and the scriptures. At a young age, the renowned ascetic, Achyuta Pragnya, initiated him into the renounced order. He was given the name "Poornapragnya" at the time of his initiation as a sanyasi.

Even as a teenager, Madhva travelled extensively in South India and gave spiritual discourses. He engaged many scholars in scriptural and philosophical debates. With this convincing reasoning, he defeated experts in tarka (logic). He was consecrated as the head of the empire of Vedant, and given the title of "Ananda Tirtha." He adopted the name Madhva to author all his works. He became famous by this name, as the founder of Tattvavada or Dwaitavada.

He attacked the existing superstitions of the time and generated intense debate. However, he also attracted a large number of followers. He travelled to Badrinath to meet the sage Ved Vyas and presented him with a commentary of the Bhagavad Geeta. After his return to Udipi, Madhvacharya wrote many commentaries. Around this time, he found a deity of Shree Krishna near the Udipi sea coast. He had the deity installed at the temple. He then undertook his second trip to Badrinath, but was asked to turn back by the Muslim armies gathered on the opposite side of the riverbank. Madhvacharya boldly crossed the river without fear for his safety. He was taken before the Muslim ruler, but he bravely declared, "I worship that Father who illuminates the entire universe; and you worship the same Father. Then why should I fear you?" His courage earned him the admiration of the Muslim king who showered him with gifts. After politely declining the gifts, he proceeded to Badrinath and met with Ved Vyas a second time. At Kurukshetra, on his way back, he is said to have found a buried mace of Bheem.

HIS WORKS

Madhvacharya wrote thirty-seven works on Dwaitavada, which are collectively referred to as the Sarvamula granthas. These include commentaries on the Bhagavad Geeta and ten Upanishads. He authored the Bhagavad Tatparya that reveals essential teachings from the Puranas. He also wrote many devotional songs. He built several temples of the Madhva sect at Udipi that are popular as pilgrimage centres even today.

Madhvacharya expounded the Dwaita school of philosophy. The tradition he began is called Sad Vaishnavism, in order to distinguish it from the Shree Vaishnavism of the Saint Ramanujacharya. According to this philosophy, Lord Vishnu is the Supreme Being, and His worship consists of (i) Ankana or marking the body with His symbols, (ii) Namakarana, using the names of the Lord and (iii) Bhajana, singing His glories.

Madhvacharya emphasised the practice of constant remembrance of God (Smarana). He said that if one forms a habit of constantly remembering the Lord at all times, it would be easy to remember Him at the time of death. Madhvacharya's Dwaita philosophy influenced the Haridasa cult, which made great contributions in the field of music and dance. Many saints later became followers of this tradition, such as Raghavendra Swami of Mantralaya. Several Mathas established in this tradition flourish to this day, and are well known for their Vedic studies as well as charitable activities.

MAHA SAMADHI

At the age of seventy-nine, Madhvacharya assigned the responsibility of carrying on the tradition of his teachings to his disciples and proceeded to Badrinath. The day on which he left for Badrinath is celebrated as Madhvanavami.

|| SANT JNANESHWAR ||

Sant Jnaneshwar was the famous author of Jnaneshwari, a Marathi commentary on the Bhagavad Geeta. He is hailed as one of the first Saints of the Bhakti movement, who influenced all Saints born in Maharashtra after him.

EARLY YEARS

Sant Jnaneshwar was born in Alandi, a small village near Pune in 1275 A.D. Jnaneshwar's father Vitthal Pant was a very religious man and had no interest in worldly attractions. His mother, Rukminibai, was very pure and was very devoted to her husband. Vitthal Pant had so much love for God that he left his wife and went off to Benaras to take up sanyas under Swami Ramananda. His wife found it very difficult to live without him. Swami Ramananda came to know of her pain and instructed Vitthal Pant to go back to Alandi to fulfill his worldly duties.

Vitthal Pant followed his Guru's instructions and returned to his wife. However, the couple was shunned by the orthodox society, as Vitthal Pant had broken the rules of sanyas. They began to mistreat the family and look upon his children as social outcasts. Vitthal Pant and Rukminibai had four children: the eldest was Nivrittinath, the second was Jnanadev, the third was Sopana, and the youngest was a daughter, Muktabai. The couple tried very hard to have their children accepted by the society, but their efforts failed. In frustration, both of them committed suicide in the river Indriyani.

THE TURNING POINT

The death of their parents made it very difficult for the children. Jnaneshwar was only nine years old at that time. Before the parents died, Jnaneshwar and his brother Nivrittinath had studied the scriptures from their father. Now after their death, Jnaneshwar made it a goal to wear the holy thread in respect of his parents' desire, who had sacrificed their lives for that purpose. He and his brothers went to Paithan to obtain a testimonial of purity, so that the sacred ceremony could be performed.

Paithan was then a center of learning. However, the priests there condemned the boys and did not allow them to meet the head priest. Jnaneshwar challenged the priests on the meaning of purity. His simple explanation of the scriptures surprised the priests, but they did not yield. They made fun of his name, which meant "Lord of Wisdom." Seeing their arrogance, Jnaneshwar quoted a verse from the Bhagavad Geeta, explaining that a God-realized person sees the Lord in every creature, be it a brahmin or an animal. The priests argued with him that if the Lord was in all creatures, then even a buffalo should be able to recite the Vedas. Jnaneshwar accepted the challenge. He walked over to a nearby buffalo and placed his hand on the buffalo's head. Much to the surprise of the priests, the buffalo started chanting the Vedic mantras. The head priest witnessed this too and without any questions gave Jnaneshwar the purity letter, and the thread ceremony was performed.

Jnaneshwar's brother Nivrittinath was once separated from the others while travelling. He entered a cave, and came upon Sant Gahinath of the Nath sect of yogis. The sage saw in Nivrittinath, a great potential yogi. He taught him Yog (yoga) for a week, in which time the Nivrittinath mastered its secrets. He then returned home and enlightened Jnaneshwar with the knowledge he had learned. He instructed Jnaneshwar to preach the message of the Bhagavad Geeta. He asked him to associate with Saints, as it was the gateway to the Lord. Jnaneshwar in turn, passed on the knowledge to the two younger siblings, Sopana and Muktabai.

INCIDENTS FROM HIS LIFE

Jnaneshwar spread the message of Krishna devotion. He often revealed himself through the miracles he performed. One day, a brahmin invited Jnaneshwar and his siblings to his home for the ceremony of the ancestors. Other priests who had also been invited did not know much the Jnaneshwar's spiritual powers, and they walked out in anger. According to them, Jnaneshwar and his siblings should not have been invited. Jnaneshwar asked the host to not worry. He invoked the hosts ancestors, who revealed themselves in the form of beautiful lights. They accepted some of the food that was offered and then disappeared after blessing the host. The other priests came to know of this and were filled of awe and admiration.

All the four children became great Saints. They shifted their residence from Alandi to Newasa, also in Maharashtra. Jnaneshwar's name spread far and wide. He and his brothers and sister traveled to various places of pilgrimage. Once in Newasa, Jnaneshwar cured a sick man called Sachindananda Baba of an incurable disease. He became a devoted disciple of Sant Jnaneshwar. From that day onwards, he took notes every time Jnaneshwar spoke.

It was here in Newasa that Janeshwar wrote a commentary on the Bhagavad Geeta, which later became famous as Jnaneshwari. After this, they returned to Alandi.

There lived, at that time, a yogi called Changdev. He was reported to be more than 400 years old, such was his mastery over the Hatha Yog techniques for controlling ageing. He was peeved that a boy like Jnaneshwar, who was barely sixteen years old at that time, was getting so much of respect. Riding on a tiger, Changdev came to Alandi with his 3000 disciples. Sant Jnaneshwar taught him a lesson by giving life to a wall and then riding on it. The Yogi was humbled and became one of Sant Jnaneshwar's foremost disciples.

Sant Jnaneshwar visited Pandarpur and had darshan of Lord Panduranga. He wrote a book called Amritnubhava. He wrote songs called abhangas. He also wrote songs for daily recitation, called Haripatha (lessons on Lord Hari).

HIS TEACHINGS

Jnaneshwar is regarded as the founder of the bhakti school of thought in Maharashtra. He always taught in Marathi. He taught that one could worship God even while sincerely doing one's duty. It was not necessary to leave the house to go in search of God. He also taught that caste was meaningless. What mattered was real devotion to God. He preached three steps of sadhana – worship the Guru, associate with Saints, and chant the name of God. The poor and simple people of rural Maharashtra were very moved by his teachings and were inspired to devotion. They began calling him Sant Jnaneshwar (Sant means Saint).

MAHA SAMADHI

At the young age of twenty-five, Sant Jnaneshwar, with permission from the Lord, took Samadhi in a cave in Alandi in 1296 A.D. He sat in a lotus posture in meditation holding his japa-mala, and gave up his body, as he was reciting the ninth chapter of the Bhagavad Geeta.

|| JAYADEV GOSWAMI ||

Jayadev Goswami was a Sanskrit poet who lived in the thirteenth century A.D. in modern day Orissa. He spent most of his life in the holy city of Jagannath Puri. He was a great devotee of Shree Radha Krishna. The contribution of Jayadev to spirituality, literature and dance, is tremendous. Every year on Sankranti, there is a big fair in the memory of Jayadev in his village, with over a hundred thousand people attending.

HIS WORKS

The greatest work of Jayadev is the "Geet Govind," a lyrical poem that is organized into twelve chapters, and describes Lord Krishna's intimate pastimes. It is one of the finest examples of Sanskrit poetry and has been translated into several languages of the world. Jayadev Goswami lived in Bengal over 300 years prior to the appearance of Shree Chaitanya Mahaprabhu. It is said that Shree Chaitanya Mahaprabhu would listen to songs from the Geet Govind in devotional ecstasy.

Jayadev also wrote the famous "Dashavatar Stotram," describing ten important descensions of Lord Vishnu. This poem became the basis of many dance and drama performances. Two of the hymns composed by Jayadev are found in the Guru Granth Sahib.

INCIDENTS FROM HIS LIFE

Jayadev's parents were Bhojadev and Bamadevi, and he was born in the village of Kenduli, in the modern day district of Khurda, in Orissa. Jayadev received his education in Sanskrit poetry from a school near Konark. There are many interesting stories about the life of Jayadev. When he wanted to be closer to his Lord, he went to Puri with his friend, without any money or food. On the way he fainted of thirst. At that time, Shree Krishna Himself came to him as a cowherd boy and offered him water and milk. After guiding him to Puri, the cowherd boy mysteriously disappeared.

Jayadev would often be lost in prayers of Lord Krishna. One day, in an ecstatic mood, he had a divine vision of the blue river Yamuna flowing through scenic mountains, and of Shree Krishna sitting on the river bank, playing His flute. This gave birth to the "Geet Govind."

Another story pertains to a section of the Geet Govind that Jayadev was having trouble writing. He could not bring himself to write that the Supreme Lord would bow before Shree Radha. He went to have a bath in the afternoon, leaving his wife Padmavati to cook the offering to the deities. While he was away, Shree Krishna arrived in the guise of Jayadev and finished the section by concluding that Krishna bows His head at the lotus feet of Shree Radha. He then took the food offering from Jayadev's wife and left. On his return, Jayadev was surprised to see his wife eat before serving him the meal. On questioning her, he realized that the Lord himself had come to help him finish writing the section that he had difficulty with.

Yet another incident is related about Jayadev's wife, Padmavati. She told the queen that a true wife is one who cannot bear her husband passing away and leaves her body the moment she finds him dead. The queen decided to play a practical joke on Padmavati and told her that Jayadev was killed by a lion in the forest. After hearing this, Padmavati fainted and died. Seeing Padmavati dead the queen was horrified. Jayadev was the Guru of the king. She told the king that his Guru's wife had been killed due to a prank by her. Fearfully, the king conveyed the news to Jayadev. However, Jayadev was unperturbed and with the unshakable faith he had in God, he was able to bring her back to life.

One day after the life of Jayadev, a woman gardener was singing verses from the Geet Govind while seated in her garden, when Lord Jagannath, charmed by the music, arrived there to listen to it. While she tended to the garden, He walked behind her, joyfully listening to her singing. As a result, the Lord's body was covered with dirt and thorns. When the Utkal Raja (King of Utkal) went into the temple, he noticed the marks of dirt on the Deity of Lord Jagannath, and immediately called for an explanation from the attendants. Lord Jagannath then revealed to him, in a dream, the episode of His going to the garden to hear the music of the malini (gardener).

The Raja at once sent his men to bring the malini. The Raja then listened to the musical verses of the Geet Govind rendered by her. Greatly appreciating Jayadev's work, the Utkal Raja wrote a book himself under the same title and offered it at the lotus feet of Lord Jagannath. However, Lord Jagannath picked up the book written by the Raja and threw it away, leaving Jayadev's Geet Govind as it is. The incident hurt the Raja so deeply that he decided to jump into the sea and commit suicide. However, Lord Jagannath appeared on the scene and prevented him from doing so. The Lord pacified the Raja, assuring him that twelve shlokas (verses) composed by the Raja would be included at the beginning of the Jayadev's Geet Govind. Since then, verses from Geet Govind are recited daily at the temple of Lord Jagannath in Puri. Even today, descendants of the malini recite verses from Geet Govind regularly in the temple of Lord Jagannath.

LAST YEARS

Jayadev used to walk a long distance to bathe in a river, as it was several miles away from his house. However, due to his old age, he could not walk to the river. Astonishingly, the river came gushing to the village he lived in, and he would recite a shloka in its praise.

Jayadev spent his last few years in Vrindavan. However, before death, he returned to his village, Kenduli in Orissa.

|| SANT KABIR ||

Sant Kabir was a great poet Saint, whose writings greatly influenced the Bhakti movement of India. He firmly believed that all human beings are equal and that attaining love for God is the ultimate aim of every individual. His immense devotion and faith towards the Supreme Lord is lucidly expressed in his teachings and writings.

EARLY LIFE

There is much debate about the date of birth and early childhood of Kabir. It is said that he was born in 1398 A.D., and that his real mother was brahmin widow. However, for some reason, she abandoned him after his birth. He was found on a lotus leaf by Niru, a Muslim weaver, and his wife Nima, who brought him up with great care and affection.

Kabir's foster parents were poor but were hard working and kind people, who provided him a very loving environment. In his childhood,

Kabir saw many holy Muslim and Hindu people, and grew up near both Hindu and Muslim places of worship. He would often put a vermillion mark on his forehead and sing the name of Lord Ram. Fortunately, his parents were very tolerant and understood that he was a special child, unlike his Muslim neighbors who would often beat him up. This only made Kabir's resolve to become a spiritual teacher stronger.

MEETING HIS GURU

Kabir wanted to make Swami Ramanand his Guru, but as a low caste Muslim, he was not sure if he would be accepted. He came to know that Swamiji used to go for a bath in the river, early morning before sunrise. One day, he lay on the steps of the river, before Swamiji came. Unknowingly, in the darkness, Swami Ramanand stepped on him. In shock, Swamiji uttered "Ram! Ram!" Kabir immediately held his feet, proclaiming, "I have touched your lotus feet, and have received the Holy Name of Ram from you. You are now my Guru."

Swami Ramanand was impressed by his intellect. Being above worldly prejudice and without a care about caste and religion, he accepted Kabir as his disciple. Kabir received spiritual knowledge from his Guru for many years. During that time, he married and lived a simple life through weaving. He was very generous by nature and often gave away whatever he could to the needy. All the while, his mind would be absorbed in God. His simple approach earned him many enemies, but with time, people started flocking to him and Kabir began imparting his spiritual message to all.

HIS TEACHINGS

Kabir rejected dry rituals that were being observed without devotion by the Hindus and the Muslims. He taught that love for God was the essence of religion. He set an example of simplicity and devotion, by chanting the glories of God, while working on his loom.

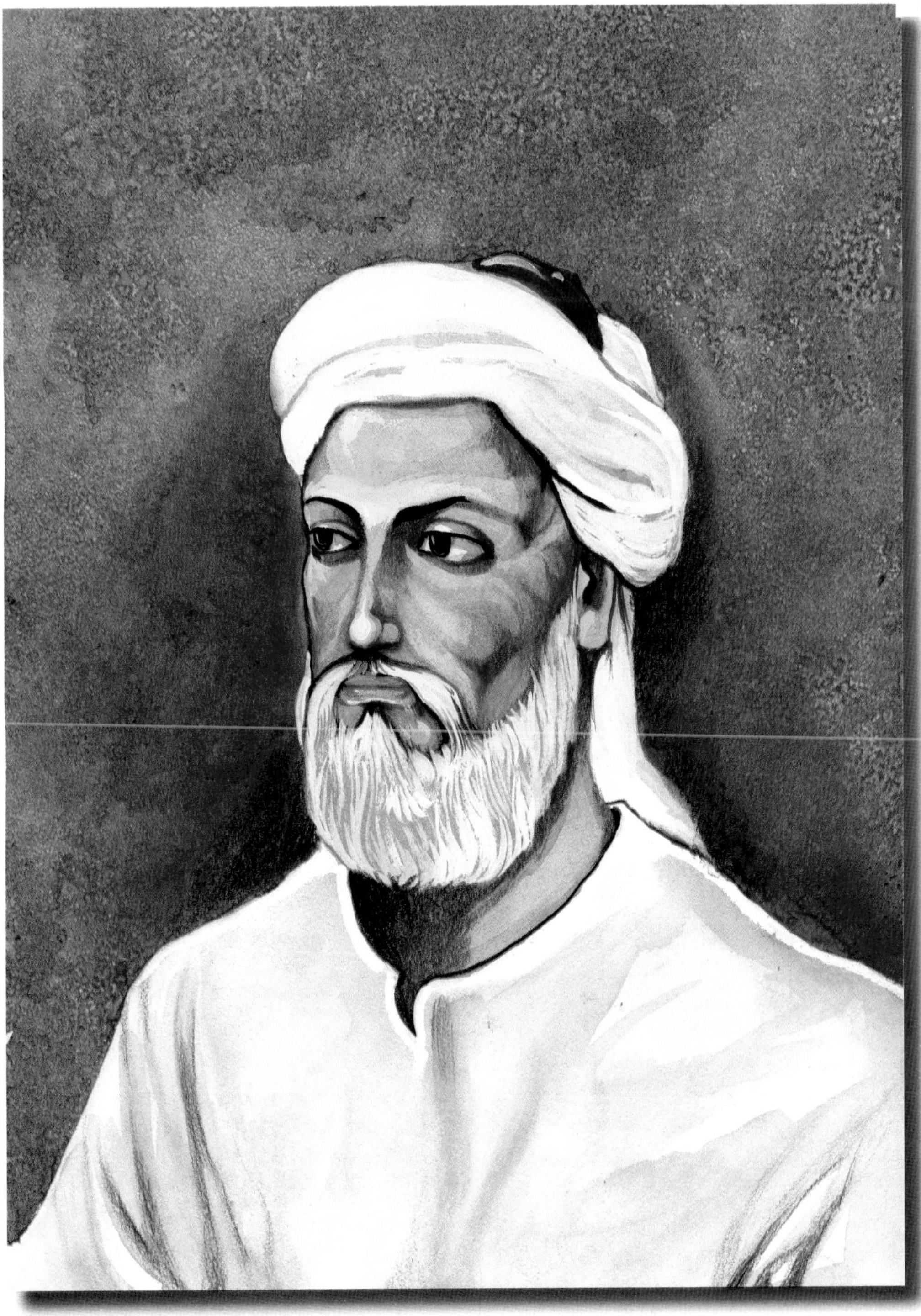

He emphasised on the oneness and unity of God, Who could be called by any name. He ridiculed those who did not preach the religion of unity and love, and sowed hatred in the name of religion. Because of his controversial teachings, Kabir was tried in the court of Sikander Lodi, the Mohammedan Ruler of Delhi, but he was able to survive all the punishments and was released subsequently.

One day, a Fakir came to see Kabir to teach him a lesson. Sensing this, Kabir tied a dirty pig to his door to prevent the fakir from entering. Unable to enter, as the fakir believed that pigs were unclean, he turned away. Kabir then asked him- "You are turning away now because I've tied an unclean pig to the door. But you have tied unclean thoughts borne of greed, anger and jealousy in your heart." The fakir fell at Kabir's feet and became his follower.

Kabir's simple teachings have made him one of the most quoted and revered poets in India by Hindus and Muslims alike. His philosophy was simple and appealing because it taught the message of goodwill and unity. His works have been collected in a book called the "Bijak," which has three categories: Sakhi, Shabad and Ramaini. The Sakhis are the most popular as they are written in simple dohas, or couplets, and deal with the experience of the soul in the world. These couplets are popular even today as "Kabir Ke Dohe." The Shabads are songs that deal with the relationship of God with the soul, and the means to attain God. Ramaini appears to have been based on Saint Tulsidas's Ramayan.

The fifth Guru of the Sikhs, Guru Arjan Dev, included over 500 verses of Kabir in the sacred Guru Granth Sahib.

THE LAST YEARS

Historians believe that Sant Kabir lived for over a hundred years and died in 1518 A.D, but some think that he died around 1448 A.D. At that time, it was widely believed that if one died in Kashi, one would attain liberation. However, before leaving his body, Kabir left Kashi and went to Maghar. He wished to instruct his disciples that the purity of the heart was important for salvation, not the place one died.

His death brought about a conflict between his Muslim and Hindu followers, who quarrelled over whether he should be given a burial or a cremation. As they removed the sheet covering Kabir's body, they were astonished to find flowers instead of the body. While one-half of the flowers were taken by his Hindu disciples, the other half was taken by his Muslim followers. Even today, Kabir's samadhi and tomb stand side-by-side.

|| GURU NANAK ||

Guru Nanak was one of the most prominent Saints of the Bhakti Movement in Medieval India. He is respected as the founder of the Sikh religion. He is also worshipped by the Sindhi community.

EARLY YEARS

Guru Nanak was born in Talwandi, a small village near Lahore, now within Pakistan, in the year 1469 A.D. His father, Mehta Kalu, was an accountant of the government administration. His mother's name was Mata Tripta Devi. He had an older sister, Bibi Nanaki, who later became his first disciple. From a very young age, Bibi Nanaki felt there was something very Divine about her brother. Guru Nanak started going to school at the age of seven.

As a young student, he narrated a beautiful verse in classical raga (melody) to his teacher. In it, he described the various stages

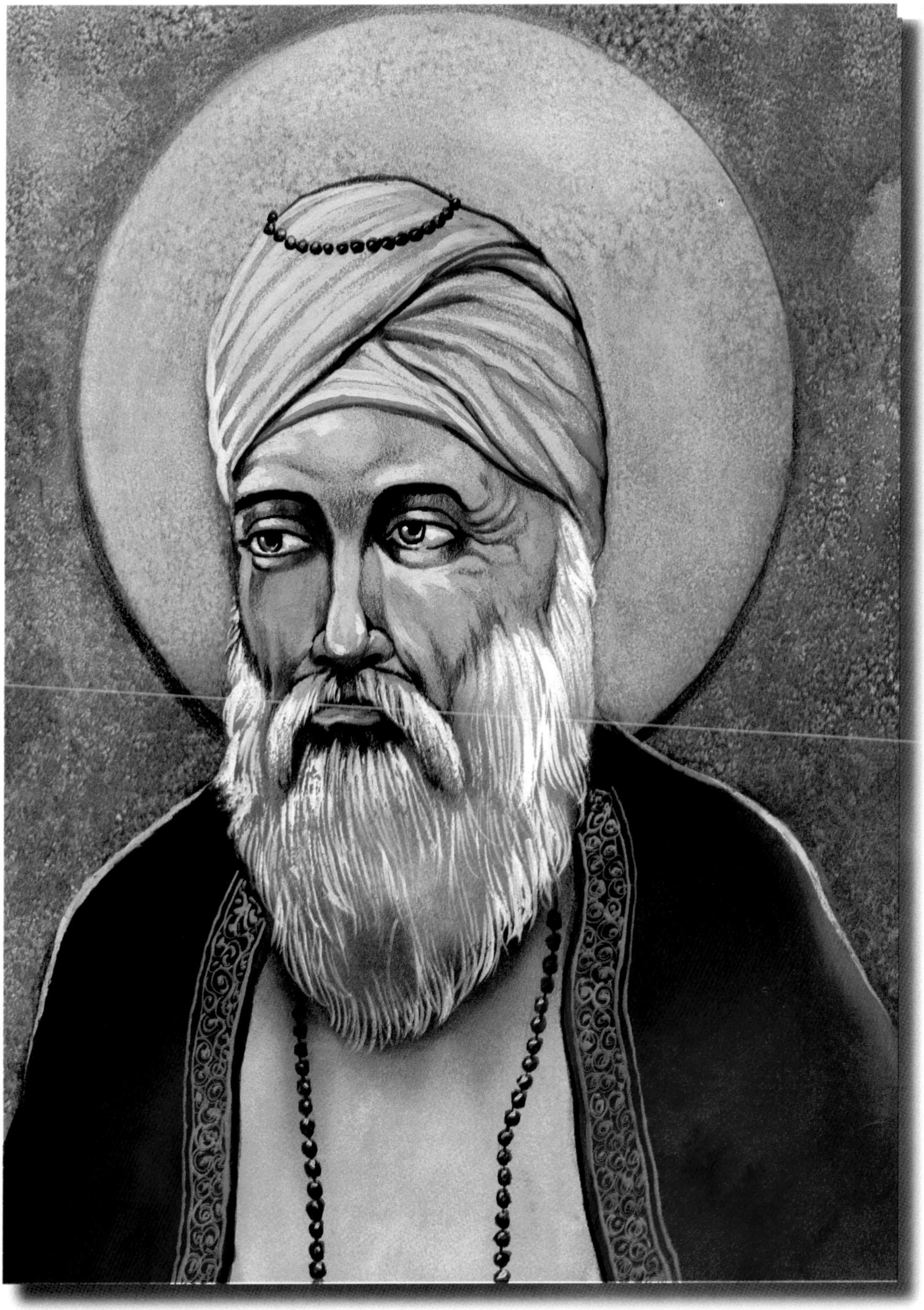

of life's spiritual journey. The teacher was so surprised that he immediately informed Guru Nanak's father about this. Guru Nanak was then sent to different schools belonging to Muslims and Hindus, to study Muslim and Hindu scriptures. He became fluent in Sanskrit, Arabic and Persian. In 1487, he got married to Sulakhani. He was blessed with two sons. At a young age, Guru Nanak heard God's voice that told him to dedicate his life to the service of humanity.

TRAVELS

To spread the message of God, Guru Nanak decided to travel across India and to other countries. For the next thirteen years, he visited various places such as Haridwar, Banaras, Gaya, Assam, Puri, Rameshwaram, Dwaraka, Delhi, Kurukshetra, Sialkot, Srinagar, Surat, Mecca, Medina, Baghdad, Pehawar, Nepal and even Tibet. He declared that Hindus and Muslims were all souls, and they all belonged to God. It was wrong to hate or condemn anyone. Everywhere he traveled, he preached his doctrine of simple devotion to God, and converted people easily to his faith.

There are many touching stories about Nanak's journeys across many countries. Once, when Nanak was in Mecca on his preaching tour, he slept with his feet pointing towards the holy shrine. When one holy man objected to it, Nanak apologized and asked him place his feet in the direction where the Lord was not present. The man was struck with wonder by Guru Nanak's insight that the Lord is present everywhere.

By the time, he returned to India, the Moghul Emperor Babur had attacked India and many civilians were being slaughtered. Guru Nanak went to Babur and convinced him to release the prisoners, and prevent further misery and bloodshed.

HIS TEACHINGS

Guru Nanak would say that remembering God always was the most important thing. We must chant God's name with every breath we take. He said this was the easiest way to reach God. While chanting God's name, the body should be engaged in selfless service. He taught that serving God's creations was the same as serving God Himself. He also taught equality and said that anyone could reach God, regardless of education, age or status. However, he warned that the road to reach God was long and that there were no shortcuts for anyone. One had to continuously purify the mind through service and chanting of God's name. Humility was very important to reach God. He taught people to throw away pride and to beg God for His grace. He was against blind superstitions and the ritualistic way of practicing religion.

HIS WORKS

Guru Nanak composed several poems. The most important one is called Japji, followed by Sohila. Japji is sung in the mornings at daybreak, while Sohila during evening prayers. These poems describe the stages of the spiritual evolution. They are included in the Guru Granth Sahib, the holy book of the Sikhs. In one of the poems, Guru Nanak explains that the essence of religion is humility, sympathy, purity and a life of goodness, and not in rituals and blind superstitious beliefs.

FINAL DAYS

Guru Nanak kept preaching until the last stage of his life. There were daily kirtans in his presence. Before leaving his material body, he appointed Guru Angad as his spiritual successor, and then covering himself with a white sheet, Guru Nanak breathed his last in 1539 A.D. After his death, both Hindus and Muslims tried to claim his body for the final rituals. When they pulled the sheet off his body, they were surprised to find flowers instead of the body.

|| CHAITANYA MAHAPRABHU ||

Chaitanya Mahaprabhu was a great Saint and devotee of Shree Krishna. He is worshipped by his followers as a descension of Shree Krishna Himself. He popularized the process of Naam Sankirtan (congregational chanting of the Names of God), which is a very simple and yet extremely powerful technique for increasing love for God.

EARLY YEARS

Chaitanya Mahaprabhu appeared on the full moon night of February 18, 1486 A.D at the time of a lunar eclipse. He was the second son of Jagannath Misra and Sachi Devi, who lived in the town of Nabadwip, in Nadia District of West Bengal.

Since he was born under a neem (margosa) tree, he was called Nimai in his childhood. He is commonly called "Gauranga" because of his exceedingly fair complexion.

When he was an infant, he would sometimes weep continuously in his mother's arms, and when the neighboring women cried "Haribol," he would stop. In this way, he made them take the name of God.

By the time he was ten, Chaitanya Mahaprabhu was well versed in Sanskrit grammar. By the age of sixteen, he developed marvellous scholarly talents. He mastered many branches of learning such as grammar, logic, literature and philosophy. Despite achieving so much at such a young age, he was very compassionate, sweet and loving. While he was still studying, his father died. On the insistence of others, he got married to Lakshmi Devi, also from Nabadwip. She died shortly after marriage from snakebite. He later got married to Vishnupriya. By this time, Chaitanya Mahaprabhu was considered a learned scholar, with debating skills second to none.

He travelled to Gaya for performing the shraadha ceremony of his father, and there he met his Guru, Ishwar Puri. This meeting transformed him completely from a scholar to a devotee. He would now constantly chant the names of Shree Krishna and dance in ecstasy. Sometimes he would be so absorbed in devotion that he would laugh, weep, fall on the ground and roll in the dust. He would cry for Lord Krishna, oblivious to his surroundings.

SANKIRTAN MOVEMENT

Nityananda (or Nitai) was an ascetic from a very young age, and wandered about in search of Krishna. When Chaitanya Mahaprabhu met Nitai, they became intimate, like brothers. Nimai instructed his devotees, Nitai and Haridas, to go from house to house, requesting everyone they met to worship and chant the names of Shree Krishna.

Jagai and Madhai were the notorious criminals in the area of Nabadwip. They plundered the rich and committed murders on the slightest provocation. They were also habitual drunkards. Nityananda decided to convert these two sinners, to reveal the glory of Chaitanya

Mahaprabhu's compassion. A procession was organized to the home of Jagai and Madhai, doing kirtan all the way. Nitai was leading the group. When he came across the two, he asked them to take Shree Krishna's name and worship Him. This angered Madhai and he attacked Nitai with a piece of a broken pot. Blood gushed from the wound.

When Chaitanya Mahaprabhu heard of the attack on Nitai by Jagai and Madhai, he flew into a rage, and wanted to kill the brothers with his Divine Chakra. Nitai begged him that these two sinners be pardoned. Moved by Nityananda's compassion on those who had hurt him, the two criminals' hearts melted, and they became disciples of Chaitanya Mahaprabhu's.

Nimai and Nitai would conduct sankirtans in various places in Nabadwip, chanting the names of Shree Radha Krishna. They would conduct religious processions, where devotees went dancing and singing through the streets. Thousands would join them and in a natural and easy way, evoke love for God within their hearts.

Since Chaitanya Mahaprabhu's mode of devotion was unconventional, the orthodox scholars began to oppose him. Chaitanya Mahaprabhu decided that if he became a sanyasi, he would win their respect, and they would accept his teachings. So at the age of twenty-four, he took sanyas from Keshav Bharati. After becoming a sanyasi, Chaitanya Mahaprabhu went to Jagannath Puri.

PASTIMES AT JAGANNATH PURI

On completing his journey from Nabadwip to Puri, when he entered the temple of Lord Jagannath, he was so overwhelmed by the Divine darshan (vision) of the Lord that he fainted in ecstasy. At that time, Sarvabhauma Bhattacharya, the most learned scholar of Puri happened to enter the temple. He saw the highest symptoms of Samadhi manifesting in the body of Chaitanya Mahaprabhu. He had Mahaprabhu's unconscious body carried to his house. Mahaprabhu returned to consciousness only when the name of "Hari" was chanted in his ears.

A debate ensued between Mahaprabhu and Sarvabhauma Bhattacharya. With utmost mastery of the Vedic scriptures and the Sanskrit language, Mahaprabhu convinced Sarvabhauma that love of God was the ultimate goal of the soul. Sarvabhauma was so impressed that from being a dry scholar he was transformed into a devotee. Chaitanya Mahaprabhu then revealed his Divinity to him, by showing him his six-armed form, with two arms of Shree Krishna (holding the flute), two arms of Shree Ram (holding the bow and arrow), and two arms of a sanyasi (holding the staff and bowl of a monk).

Mahaprabhu settled in Puri, but went on long tours from there. On one such tour, he walked all the way from Puri through South India to Dwaraka in Gujarat, and back. On this trip, he met a leper, named Vasudev. His wounds were rotting on his body, and worms had made their home in them. However, Vasudev was so kind-hearted that when a worm fell from the wound onto the ground, he would place it back in the wound. He was scared of approaching Chaitanya Mahaprabhu and offered obeisance from far. Mahaprabhu embraced him tightly, and instantly all his wounds got healed.

Mahaprabhu also went on a journey to Vrindavan, the land of Shree Krishna's pastimes. Vrindavan was overgrown by trees at that time. He revealed the glorious places of Radha and Krishna's Divine pastimes. He also instructed his disciples Rupa and Sanatana to live in Vrindavan and reveal its glories to the people. Today, Vrindavan Dham is a place of pilgrimage for millions of devotees from around the world.

In Puri, Ratha Yatra is the biggest festival. Chaitanya Mahaprabhu would celebrate it joyfully. In front of the chariot on which Lord Jagannath would be seated, he would dance with his devotees, to the accompaniment of drums and cymbals.

LATER YEARS

In his later years, Mahaprabhu stopped interacting with the people. He spent his time in a small room, called "Gambhira." All day and night, he would long to meet God, in the mood of Radharani's longing for Shree Krishna. During this period he displayed the highest levels of Divine love, that have inspired devotees ever since.

Chaitanya Mahaprabhu ended his pastimes on the earth in 1534 A.D. It is believed that he entered the temple of Lord Jagannath, and walked into the deity, merging himself with the Lord. Thus, he did not leave his mortal remains on the earth.

|| JAGADGURU VALLABHACHARYA ||

Vallabhacharya was the founder of the Pushti sect in India. He established the philosophy of Shuddha Advaita (pure non-dualism). In Indian philosophy, he is also known as the writer of sixteen stotras (tracts), as well as several commentaries on the Shreemad Bhagavatam, describing the pastimes of Lord Krishna. He was considered to be one of the five great Vaishnav acharyas of the past, who established Vaishnav schools, the others being Ramanujacharya, Madhvacharya, Nimbarkacharya and Chaitanya Mahaprabhu.

EARLY YEARS

Vallabhacharya was born in late fifteenth century A.D. at Champaranya (in Madhya Pradesh) in a Telugu brahmin household. There is a legend surrounding Vallabh's birth. He was born premature and seeing no signs of life in the baby, his parents placed him under a tree. It is believed that Lord Krishna appeared in a dream to his parents and reassured them that

their child was Divine. The parents rushed to the spot and found the baby alive, and protected by a circle of fire. They named him "Vallabh," which means "dear one" in Sanskrit.

Vallabh commenced studying the scriptures at the age of seven with the study of the four Vedas. He lost his father when he was only eleven years old. At the age of twelve, he was able to complete the study of the Vedas, the six Darshans and the eighteen Puranas. He also learned the philosophic systems of Shankaracharya, Nimbarkacharya, Ramanujacharya and Madhvacharya, along with the Buddhist and Jain schools. He was able to recite hundreds of mantras, not only from beginning to end, but also in the reverse order. This won him the title of "Bal Saraswati."

VICTORY AT VIJAYANAGAR

Vallabh attended the court of Raja Krishnadevaraya of Vijayanagar and debated with the court pundits. The philosophical question under debate was whether God is dualistic or non-dualistic. The discussion continued for twenty-seven days. Vallabh turned out victorious and the Raja was so pleased that he showered Vallabh with wealth and bestowed upon him the title of "Acharya." Vallabhacharya distributed most of the wealth and set forth on travels to many places.

HIS TRAVEL

Vallabhacharya went on three pilgrimages of India barefooted. He wore a simple white dhoti and a white covering cloth to cover the upper part of his body. He lectured on the Shreemad Bhagavatam and discoursed on it in 84 places. These places are still visited by pilgrims and are referred to as Chaurasi Bethak. He would stay in Braj for four months in a year.

It is believed that when Vallabhacharya entered Gokul, Lord Krishna appeared in the form of Shreenathji and disclosed a verse, Shree Krishna Sharanam Mama, for dedication to the Lord. Vallabhacharya then began preaching the path of devotion and Grace, called the Pushti Marg. Thousands became his disciples, but 84 devoted servants are the most famous, and their lives have been documented in Pushti Marg literature as "The Story of 84 Vaishnavs."

Vallabhacharya remained a celibate for long. However, Vitthalnath of Pandharpur, commanded him to marry and live the life of a householder. Obeying, he married Mahakanya and had sons, Gopinath and Vitthalnath.

HIS WORKS

The important works of Vallabhacharya include Sanskrit texts like the Vyas Sutra Bhashya, Jaimini Sutra Bhashya and the Siddhant Rahasya. He also wrote extensively in Braj bhasha (the language of Braj).

Vallabhacharya contributed significantly to the essence of philosophical thought during the Bhakti movement of the middle ages. The unique aspect of the sect established by Vallabhacharya is that it promotes devotion to Lord Krishna in His child form. This ideology, called Pushti Marg, has grown very vast in present times. In the last five centuries, immense art, culture and music has been inspired by this tradition.

LAST DAYS

According to Pushti literature, in 1530 A.D, Shreenathji asked Vallabhacharya to leave worldly life and come near Him. The Lord had expressed this wish on two previous occasions as well. Vallabhacharya took the third command as the final verdict. He then went to Kashi and took sanyas with a vow of silence. He lived in a hut made of leaves on the Hanuman ghat, and contemplated on Lord Krishna. His family assembled to see him for the last time and asked him for advice. Vallabhacharya scribbled the Sanskrit verses in sand, which are known as Shiksha Shloki. He immersed himself in the River Ganga on the day of Rath Yatra. The people assembled then saw a bright flame that ascended to the sky. This episode is known as Asura Vyamohan Leela.

|| NARSI MEHTA ||

Narsi Mehta was a poet Saint, and his bhajan, Vaishnav Jana To Tene Kahiye, was popularized by Mahatma Gandhi. He is especially revered in Gujarat, where he is acclaimed as the Adi Kavi, or first poet, who set the base for Gujarati literature.

Narsi Mehta was a devotee of Lord Krishna right from his childhood. He was unmindful of his worldly affairs, being ever intoxicated by devotion. He obtained the Divine vision of Lord Krishna on multiple occasions.

EARLY YEARS

Narsi Mehta was born in early fifteenth century A.D. in Junagadh, Gujarat in an orthodox Brahmin family. When Narsi was very young, he did not speak for a long time and his parents were worried that he might be mute. One day, he was taken by his parents to a saint at the Krishna temple. The saint told Narsi to repeat Shree Krishna's name, which happened to be the first words uttered by the child.

At a young age, Narsi lost his parents and went to live with his uncle. His grandmother took him to see temples and to meet Saints who visited the holy shrines.

Narsi was not drawn to studies and schooling. Instead, he preferred to listen to spiritual discourses. He was enraptured by the story of Lord Krishna. He would dress himself as Radha or a gopi, and dance frequently. Narsi married Menakabai and had a daughter and a son.

TURNING POINT

Once, Narsi ran away from his house after a disagreement with his sister-in-law and went to a forest where he found an abandoned Shiv temple. Tired and hungry, Narsi embraced the Shivling tightly and prayed to the Lord to protect him. He fell asleep while chanting the names of the Lord. When he opened his eyes, he found Lord Shiv before him asking him what he wanted. Narsi replied that he wanted whatever was most dear to Lord Shiv. Lord Shiv made the forest disappear and in its place was a beautiful garden where Lord Krishna was playing with the gopis. Lord Krishna took a tulsi leaf from His garland and put it in Narsi's mouth. As his hunger disappeared, Narsi was overjoyed with the outpouring of sacred songs from deep within. Lord Krishna blessed him saying that he would spread devotion everywhere. In the meantime, Narsi's uncle found him at the temple and took him home.

INCIDENTS FROM HIS LIFE

When his daughter was of a marriageable age, Menakabai worried that they did not have enough money for her wedding. She asked Narsi to request some rich people for help. However, Lord Krishna Himself came to Narsi in his dreams, asking him to send a hundi (a letter of request for money) to Seth Samaldas in Dwaraka, who would hand over the money. Narsi immediately sent a hundi for Rs. 1500 to a messenger's house, as he could then travel to Dwarka to get the

money. At that time, some merchants were present at the messenger's house, who were planning to go to Dwaraka. They offered to give Narsi the money and collect it from Seth Samaldas in Dwaraka. Narsi was thus able to get his daughter married in a grand fashion.

The merchants went to Dwaraka and unable to find Seth Samaldas, they were upset and thought that Narsi had deceived them. After a while, a man approached the merchants saying he was Seth Samaldas and gave them Rs. 2000. He said that the extra money was a reward to them for helping Narsi. Thus, Lord Krishna Himself came to help His devotee in the form of Seth Samaldas.

Narsi had to face many charges from his community and was tried in the Raja's temple. However, a miracle took place, when the temple doors opened and a garland fell around the neck of Narsi. All the people, including the Raja were astounded by the extent of Narsi's devotion to his Lord. They dropped the charges against him.

HIS TEACHINGS

Narsi believed in living simply, and gave away all his money to the poor and needy. Although he had to face many problems from his brother's wife, he was always gracious. He felt that his adversity had truly helped him in getting a vision of the Lord.

He became very famous for his bhajans and people came from long distances to hear them. He always preached love for Lord Krishna. He also tried to bring the Shiv and Vaishnav sects together through his teachings that the two were essentially the same. Narsi did not believe in caste differences and although he was a brahmin, he respected and became friends with people of all social statuses. He frequently held prayer sessions in the houses of people from lower social status. This annoyed his brahmin community.

Once in a brahmin community feast, he was questioned about his behavior. However, a miracle took place, where every brahmin member found a member of lower caste seated next to them. Narsi thus came to be accepted by all and was acknowledged as a great saint.

Narsi described in his bhajans that a true Vaishnava was one who possessed qualities of kindness towards all, righteousness, love for God, and truthfulness. In his life, he displayed these virtues abundantly.

MAHA SAMADHI

Narsi Mehta died in late fifteenth century A.D. Throughout his life, he showed people the path of true devotion and he continues to inspire millions, centuries after his death.

|| SOORDAS ||

Soordas was a great poet Saint during the time of the Bhakti movement in India. He is renowned for his compositions in praise of Lord Krishna, which number in thousands. His name literally means "servant of devotional melody," and his songs are popular even today.

EARLY YEARS

Soordas was born in the district of Mathura in Uttar Pradesh, in a poor family. He was blind from birth, and hence during his childhood, he received harsh treatment from his family. At the age of six, a group of devotional musicians passed by his home. He followed them and left his home forever.

When he was eighteen, he had the good fortune of meeting his Spiritual Master, Vallabhacharya, on the banks of the River Yamuna.

Mahaprabhu Vallabhacharya was a great devotee of Lord Krishna, who was travelling throughout India, preaching the glories of devotion to the Lord. Vallabhacharya accepted Soordas as his disciple and taught him the secrets of the scriptures. From him, Soordas learned the path of devotion, called Pushti Marg. He studied the Shreemad Bhagavatam under the guidance of his Guru, and immersed himself in Divine love of Shree Krishna.

Soordas had such an excellent memory that he memorized the entire Bhagavatam, consisting of 18,000 verses. Since he was musically inclined, his Guru asked him to sing the leelas (pastimes) of Shree Radha Krishna from the Bhagavatam. Seeing his exceptional ability to sing and inspire devotees, he was appointed the resident singer of the Shreenathji temple in Govardhan.

HIS WORKS

During the 14th to 17th centuries, a great bhakti movement spread throughout India. Many Saints were born throughout India, who taught the people to cast aside the heavy burden of ritualism and philosophic subtleties, and simply absorb themselves in overwhelming love for God. These bhakti Saints wrote an extensive amount of literature in the local languages of the various States of India. Soordas is credited with giving the Bhakti movement a big boost through his simple style of singing melodious songs describing the beautiful pastimes of the Lord. His compositions are imbued with the sweet bliss of Divine love to Shree Radha Krishna. It is almost as if he was able to see the pastimes of Shree Radha Krishna and describe them so beautifully in his works.

He was responsible for many great compositions, the chief ones being the Soor Sagar (Ocean of Melody), Soor Saravali (songs based on the festival of Holi) and the Sahitya Lahiri (songs glorifying devotion towards the Supreme Lord). Soordas's unique style sparked off a "Soor tradition." The word "Soor" came to mean blind person, and many blind poets who came after him, signed their compositions as "Soor."

The Guru Granth Sahib, the Holy book of the Sikhs, also has several of his works called the Soordas Bani. It is said that Guru Arjan Dev, the fifth Guru of the Sikhs, created compositions in accordance with the style of Soordas. He has referred to Soordas as Bhagat, and has held him in reverence.

LAST YEARS

Soordas never got married, and he spent the latter part of his life in singing the glory of his Lord and giving lectures on devotion. His singing brought him fame from far and wide and Emperor Akbar became his patron. He lived a simple life until his death in the late sixteenth century.

Soordas's innumerable melodious compositions are testimony to his greatness as they inspire devotees even today on the path of bhakti.

|| SANT EKNATH ||

Sant Eknath was one of the greatest saints of Maharashtra. His big contribution to the society was the spreading of Sanatan Dharma (Eternal Religion) and its philosophy down to the common person. .

EARLY YEARS

He was born in Paithan, Maharashtra in 1533 A.D. Paithan is a revered as a holy place, and in those days, it was a center of Sanskrit learning. His parents died when he was only three years old, and his grandparents raised him. His great grandfather, Sant Bhanudas, was a well-known saint.

At a young age, Eknath became a disciple of Janardana Swami, who lived near his town. Janardana Swami taught him Sanskrit grammar, philosophy and texts from the holy books. Eknath also studied the Jnaneshwari, Sant Jnandeva's commentary on the Bhagavad Geeta.

On his Guru's instructions, Eknath was married to Girijabai from Bijapur and settled into household life. His wife was a very religious woman and proved to be a great companion and support to Eknath. He is a great example of a Saint who effectively blended worldly life and spiritual progress. Even though he lived in the world, he was not attached to it.

HIS WORKS

Once Eknath's education was complete, he accompanied his Guru on a pilgrimage. At a place near Nasik, they heard a discourse on the Shreemad Bhagavatam in Sanskrit. Janardana Swami asked Eknath to translate what they had heard into Marathi, and to write his own commentary, so that ordinary people would understand it. Eknath followed his Guru's advice and the result was the "Chatusloki Bhagavat," his first work. Eknath attributed this and all his later works to his Guru's inspiration, but signing the books as 'Eka-Janardana' (Eknath of Janardana).

His most important work is the Eknathi Bhagavat. After the first five chapters were written, one of his disciples took them to Varanasi. He was reciting them on the banks of the river Ganges. The pundits heard that and were very angry because they felt that the holy books should only be read in Sanskrit and not in any other language. They called Eknath to Varanasi and asked for an explanation. Eknath requested them to listen to his work before they decided on a punishment. Reluctantly, they agreed. The chief Pundit kept a curtain between him and Eknath because he was scared he might be polluted by Eknath. When Eknath started reciting his poems, the pundits were very impressed with the melody and they found the philosophy very clear and moving. Towards the end, they were ecstatic. The chief Pundit tore down the curtain and asked Eknath to complete the work in Varanasi on the banks of the Ganges.

Apart from that Eknath wrote many other texts, such as Rukmini Swayamvar, Bhavarth Ramayan and Shukashtak. In 1584 A.D.,

Eknath completed editing the Jnaneshwari. The version we read today is his edited version.

He spent his time in his devotional works. He wrote a number of songs and poems, besides devotional and philosophical works.

HIS TEACHINGS

Eknath was well versed in Sanskrit, Arabic, Urdu, Persian, Hindi and Marathi. In order to make sure that people understood him, Eknath preached in Marathi and not Sanskrit. He emphasized singing and chanting bhajans and the name of the Lord. He taught people about the importance of virtuous conduct, meditation and sincerity in performing duties. He spoke about seeing God everywhere and in everything.

In his lifetime, he wrote various commentaries, poems and kirtans. Almost all his writings were in Marathi. He even introduced a new form of Marathi religious songs called Bharood. He started a movement in Maharashtra called Vasudeva Sanstha. It involved individuals visiting households and conveying religious messages through bhajans, which were sung at the doors of their homes.

PRACTICAL LESSONS

Eknath was very famous in his village because of his patience, and it was said that nothing could make him angry. Once, a vagabond heard about Eknath's patience and decided to prove to the others that Eknath could get angry just like ordinary humans. The next morning, after Eknath was returning from his bath in the river Narmada, the vagabond spat on Eknath. Instead of getting angry, Eknath simply turned back and went to bathe again. As he came out of the river, the vagabond was waiting, and spat on him once again. Again, Eknath did not get angry and returned to the river for another bath. This went on for a while. Each time, the vagabond would spit, Eknath would return to the river, without losing his temper. Finally, the vagabond gave up and asked Eknath how it was possible for him to be like this. Eknath was full of love and compassion and replied, "Brother, you are my well wisher. It is because of you that I have bathed so many times in the holy Narmada today. Why should I become angry with you?" The vagabond was so touched and he became a changed man from that day onwards.

Besides the orthodox priests, even Eknath's son, Hari, did not agree with his different way of thinking. Hari was a pundit and did not approve of his father preaching in Marathi and eating in homes of socially backward people. When Eknath found out of his son's resentment, he agreed to change his ways (with a heavy heart), for the sake of his son. Hari would give discourses in Sanskrit, while Eknath would remain quiet. Very soon, nobody was coming to the lectures as people were dying for Eknath's kirtans and discourses. Hari realized his folly and asked for forgiveness. From that day onwards, Eknath started preaching again.

MAHA SAMADHI

Eknath left his mortal body in 1599 A.D.

|| TULSIDAS ||

Tulsidas is the famous writer of the Ramcharitmanas, the Hindi Ramayana. He also wrote several works of great religious significance. He is widely regarded as the reincarnation of the sage Valmiki.

In the Bhavishyottar Puran, Lord Shiva narrates to Parvati how Valmiki received a boon from Hanuman to enable him to sing the glories of Lord Rama in Kaliyug. It is believed that Tulsidas thus came to fulfil the prophecy.

EARLY YEARS

Tulsidas was born on the auspicious day of Shravan shukla (bright fortnight) saptami, in the middle of the sixteenth century A.D. at the time of the Mughal Emperor Akbar's reign. He was born to a brahmin family in Banda district of Uttar Pradesh.

Tulsidas was married at a young age to Ratnavali. The story goes that Tulsidas was extremely attached to his wife and was unable to bear separation from her when she once went to her father's house for a visit. He therefore went to see his wife stealthily in the middle of the night. Her father's house was across the river, and it was a stormy night, so no boatman was willing to take Tulsidas across. In his desperation to meet his wife, Tulsidas used a piece of log to cross the river. He then found a rope hanging from the second floor of the house, and used it to climb into his wife's bedroom. Ratnavali was shocked to find her husband coming to meet her in the middle of such a stormy night. She asked him how he had come, and Tulsidas told her about the log and the rope.

When she peeped out of the window, she discovered that the log was actually a floating corpse, and the rope was a snake that had been climbing the wall. Ratnavali rebuked Tulsidas saying she was only a bag of flesh and bones, and if he had a similar level of attachment for Lord Ram, he would have crossed the ocean of maya and attained salvation. Stung by her words, Tulsidas left his wife and young son and became an ascetic. He wandered around for fourteen years visiting various places of pilgrimage.

HIS WORKS

Tulsidas is most famous for the Ramcharitmanas. Although written primarily in Awadhi language, it also incorporates several local languages such as Brijbhasha, Bhojpuri and the local dialect of Chitrakoot. Like the original Ramayan in Sanskrit, the Ramcharitmanas is held in great reverence in Northern India, and is sung to innumerable melodious tunes. Many of its verses have become popular quotations in North India.

In addition to this, Tulsidas wrote several other works such as the Dohavali, Kavitavali, Geetavali, Vinay Patrika and hymns in praise of Lord Ram and Hanuman. Of these, the Hanuman Chalisa is especially popular.

HIS TEACHINGS

Tulsidas's doctrine teaches contemplation on the Name, Form, Virtues, Pastimes, Abode and Associates of Lord Ram. As the Lord

Himself lives in His Name, chanting the Name is a powerful means of developing devotion towards Him. One must surrender to Lord Ram, and pursue devotion to Him, without any consideration of self-interest. Saint Tulsidas never founded any school of followers, nor did he take the position of Guru. However, his teachings have had a profound influence on the people of North India.

INCIDENTS FROM HIS LIFE

There is an interesting story associated with Ramcharitmanas. It is said that once some thieves went to Tulsidas's ashram with the intention of stealing the great work. They were unable to enter as there were two blue-complexioned guards at the gate with bows and arrows. During the day, when the thieves confessed this to him, Tulsidas wept on the realization that Lord Ram and Lakshman had themselves come to protect his work.

Another legend goes that once Tulsidas went to Vrindavan and visited a temple of Lord Krishna. On seeing the idol, he was moved by the beauty but expressed his inability to offer obeisance to the Diety as he could only bow his head in front of Lord Ram. The Lord revealed himself in the form of Lord Ram with bow and arrows to fulfil his devotee's desire. Thus, He conveyed the powerful message that Lord Krishna and Lord Ram are the same Supreme God.

It is said that once Tulsidas brought back to life the husband of a poor woman. When news reached the Mughal emperor at Delhi, Tulsidas was taken prisoner and ordered to perform a miracle to save his own life. Tulsidas humbly replied that he had no special powers and was only a devotee of Lord Ram. Tulsidas prayed to Hanuman and when armies of monkeys entered the royal palace, the king had to admit defeat.

MAHASAMADHI

Tulsidas is believed to have left for his worldly abode sometime in the early seventeenth century A.D. at the age of ninety-one, in Kashi.

|| MEERABAI ||

Meerabai was a poet Saint belonging to a dignified family of Rajasthan. From an early age Meerabai felt an irresistible attraction and devotion to Shree Krishna. Meerabai abandoned everything in her quest of devotion to Lord Krishna. She chose the life of simplicity and became a well-known Saint of her time. She demonstrated ideals of fearlessness, grace and steadfastness in the face of severe odds. Her greatest contribution was through her compositions as she was a gifted poet. In a simple, lucid style, she was able to express her deep love for her Lord through hundreds of poems that are sung even today.

EARLY YEARS

Meerabai was born in the early sixteenth century A.D. Her father, Ratan Singh Rathore, was the son of the founder of the city of Jodhpur. Meera's mother and grandfather died when she was very young and she grew up to be a quiet and thoughtful child. When Meera was just five years old, a saint visited their house in Vrindavan. Meera was deeply impressed by the saint and followed him around. The saint realized that this was no ordinary child and as a parting gift, he gave Meera a small deity of Lord Krishna, which she preserved with great dedication.

LIFE CHANGING EVENT

Once, when she was a small girl, Meera watched a wedding procession go by and out of curiosity, she asked her mother where her bridegroom was. Her mother took her to the prayer room and pointing to Lord Krishna's idol, told her that He was her bridegroom. This left a lasting impact on Meera as she left her playful pursuits and started loving the deity of Giridhar Gopal as her husband. As Meera grew up to be a beautiful young woman, her love for Lord Krishna remained steadfast.

HER MARRIAGE

Her marriage was arranged to prince Bhojraj who was the heir to the throne of Chittorgarh, and the eldest son of the famous Rajput king, Rana Sangha. Although she was wed into a prestigious family, Meera never took the marriage seriously. She carried with her as dowry, the deity of Lord Krishna, which she worshipped as if it embodied the living presence of Krishna. She felt she was truly married to Shree Krishna. Her new family did not approve of her piety and devotion, especially when she refused to worship the family deity in place of Shree Krishna.

Meera's husband died in a battle. This probably strengthened her decision not to love material personalities, and she turned all her affection to the spiritual realm. Her passionate spiritual devotion inspired her to compose hundreds of songs filled with love for God.

In the beginning, Meera kept her devotion to Shree Krishna private. Later, she cast away her shyness, and would dance in ecstasy, while singing the bhajans in the temples and the streets. Her brother-in-law,

Rana Vikramjit was the new ruler of Chittorgarh. He strongly objected to Meera's popularity, her mixing with commoners and her lack of feminine shyness.

There were several attempts to poison her. Once, Rana Vikramjit gave her a bowl of poison, saying that it was the charanamrita of Giridhar Gopal. Meera drank with a smile and her Lord's name on her lips. The sight of her dancing astounded everyone and singing the glories of her Lord, as the poison had no effect on her.

INCIDENTS FROM HER LIFE

On one occasion, Emperor Akbar came in disguise to see Meera. Accompanied by Tansen, Akbar became enchanted by the songs of Meera and fell at her feet in obeisance. Enraged that she had allowed a Muslim to touch her feet, the Rana asked Meera to drown in the river. As she was about to jump, a hand pulled her back from behind. As she turned around, she realized that it was Lord Krishna who had saved her, and she fainted. When she recovered, the Lord told her that she did not need to live with her in-laws anymore, and that she should go to Vrindavan.

In Vrindavan, Meera desired to meet the saint Jeev Goswami, who was respected as the most senior devotee of Shree Krishna residing there. She requested his attendants outside to let her in, to meet Jeev Goswami. However, being a sanyasi, Jeev Goswami refused to see her, saying that it was his personal rule not to speak to women. On hearing this from his attendants, Meera boldly replied, "I thought there was only one male in Vrindavan. Who is this second male who says he does not speak to women?" When Meera's reply was conveyed to Jeev Goswami, he was shocked! He realized that he was still at the platform of the body, where he distinguished between men and women. However, Meera was at a much higher level of realization, where she was seeing herself and all others as the souls. Jeev Goswami came running out to greet Meerabai, and personally brought her into the house.

LAST DAYS

People started flocking to see Meera as the story of her devotion spread.

As Meera realized that her end was near, she decided to go and live in Dwaraka, the other holy land of Shree Krishna. There, she would sing bhajans daily for Lord Dwarakadhish, in the temple. Her brother-in-law, Rana Vikramjit, repented that he had troubled such a great devotee of the Lord, and so misfortune had befallen his kingdom. He came to meet Meera in Dwaraka, and requested her to return to Chittorgarh. Meera was in the temple at that time. She got up and walked towards the deity of Lord Dwarakadhish, saying, "O Giridhari! You are calling me. Leaving You, where can I go; I am coming to You." She walked into the garbha griha (sanctum sanctorum), and miraculously the doors were shut. When they opened, Meera was nowhere to be seen. Her saree was wrapped around the deity; her mortal frame had merged into her Divine Beloved.

Meerabai is famous the world over. To this day, people are inspired by the path of devotion shown by Meerabai in the pursuit of Divine love. Her intense love and longing for a vision of Shree Krishna took her to the pinnacle of bhakti.

|| SANT TUKARAM ||

Sant Tukaram was a great poet Saint of India and made huge contributions to the Bhakti Movement in Maharashtra. Tukaram is considered the most influential figure in the history of Marathi literature. He was a devotee of Lord Vitthal (a form of Shree Krishna). He is especially revered by the Varkari community.

EARLY YEARS

Tukaram was born in Maharashtra in the early seventeenth century. There is dispute over the exact date of his birth, as some historians put the date closer to late sixteenth century. Tukaram started supporting his family at a very early age due to his father's illness. Soon after his parents' death, Tukaram was faced with hardships. He lost his wife Rakhumabai very early in life.

He remarried and with his second wife, he had three sons. It is said that he was persecuted by his second wife to the extent that he went into depression. At this time, he had a dream that proved to be the turning point. Chaitanya Mahaprabhu came in his dream, and initiated him into the spiritual path. That moment started his journey as a poet Saint.

HIS WORKS

Tukaram was a devotee of Vitthala, a deity form of Lord Krishna worshipped in Maharashtra. Like other famous Bhakti Saints (Namdev, Eknath and Janabai) of Maharashtra, Tukaram has composed several thousand abhangs (devotional songs) in his mother tongue, Marathi. These abhangs usually consist of four couplets, of which the second couplet generally contains the theme of the poem. Tukaram's abhangs are a devotional treasure of the Bhakti Movement of Maharashtra.

Tukaram is credited with the work Gatha, which is a collection of 4500 abhangs. He was also was responsible for a Marathi translation of the Bhagavad Geeta in abhang form that brings out the devotional facet of the scripture. Tukaram's teachings found their way into the Guru Granth Sahib, as the Sikhs appreciated the enlightened writings of Tukaram.

Several miracles are attributed to Tukaram. It is believed that once when the local brahmins forced him to throw his manuscripts into the river Indrayani, Tukaram undertook a fast unto death. On the thirteenth day, the manuscripts reappeared and his enemies had to accept defeat. Incidents like these made him famous and he came to be known as Sant Tukaram.

HIS TEACHINGS

Tukaram preached that we should make God the center of our life. He taught that to attain God, it is not necessary to renounce the world and lead an ascetic life. He preached simplicity in devotion to the Lord. He firmly abhorred elaborate rituals that were in abundance in those days. He considered mystic powers as impediments in the attainment of genuine devotion. He emphasised the need for serving fellow beings with love as a means of serving the Lord. Tukaram also advocated the chanting of the Lord's name. His teachings were very broad-based and he worked for the upliftment of society. Hence the Varkari tradition in Maharashtra emphasizes the need for community service and group worship.

LATER YEARS

Sant Tukaram sang in public with fourteen accompanists in the Varkari tradition of the Bhakti Movement. To this day, his songs are popular, although his original works have not been completely preserved. It is said that when Tukaram was forty-two years old, he disappeared. His devout followers believed that Lord Vitthal Himself carried Tukaram away.

|| TYAGARAJA ||

Tyagaraja was one of the greatest composers of the Carnatic music tradition. He was an inexhaustible writer, with thousands of devotional compositions in his name. Most of these were written in glorification of Lord Ram. Five of his compositions are particularly popular even today and are called Panchartna Kritis (five gems). He is considered one of the trinity in the Carnatic school of music, the others being Muthuswamy Dikshitar and Shyama Shastri.

EARLY YEARS

Tyagaraja was born in 1759 in Tiruvayur (Tanjavur district of modern day Tamil Nadu), in a Telugu brahmin household. Tyagaraja was named after Lord Tyagaraja, the presiding Deity of his town. His maternal grandfather was a poet composer in the court of the king of Tanjavur. Tyagaraja was married at a young age but lost his wife and remarried later in life.

Even at an early age, Tyagaraja's innate talent was evident. He began composing songs when he was only eight years old. He regarded music as a way of experiencing God's love. His objective while composing would be purely devotional, as opposed to focusing on the technicalities of classical music. In his teens, he composed his first song, Namo Namo Raghavaya, in the Desika Todi raag. A couple of years later, he composed and sang one of the songs of the Pancharatna Kritis. Impressed by this, his music teacher informed the King of Tanjavur about his pupil's amazing talent. The king invited Tyagaraja to visit his court and sing in his presence. As Tyagaraja was not inclined towards a life in court and preferred to spend time composing songs glorifying the Lord, he declined. On this occasion, he composed a song that questions whether wealth is happiness. The king, unable to sustain his curiosity, went in disguise to Tyagaraja's house to see the musical genius. Angered by the rejection of the royal offer, Tyagaraja's brother threw the idol of Lord Ram into the nearby Cauvery river. Losing his Lord proved unbearable to Tyagaraja and he went on various pilgrimages to temples in South India composing many beautiful devotional songs in the process. It is said that Lord Ram appeared in a dream to him and told him where to find the deity. He is said to have found the deity of his beloved Lord Ram at exactly the same place as described in the dream within five days.

HIS WORKS

Any discussion of Carnatic music would remain incomplete without mention of Tyagaraja. He is said to have written 600 Kritis (compositions) and musical plays in Telugu. He is credited with over 24,000 Kritis in praise of Lord Ram. Although Tyagaraja was interested in music as a means of experiencing devotional love of God, he made immense contributions leading to technical development in this school of music. More than 200 years later, concerts in Carnatic music still resound with his melodious and devotional song compositions.

MAHA SAMADHI

He is believed to have attained Samadhi around 1847 A.D.

|| SHREE RAMAKRISHNA PARAMHANSA ||

Shree Ramakrishna Paramhansa was a famous saint of 19th-century India. His religious philosophy led to the formation of the Ramakrishna Mission by his chief disciple Swami Vivekananda. Many of his disciples believe he was an incarnation of God. Born in a brahmin Vaishnav family in rural Bengal, he became a priest of the Dakshineshwar Kali Temple. Though conventionally uneducated, he attracted the attention of numerous Bengali intellectuals.

EARLY YEARS

Shree Ramakrishna was born in a small village in Bengal called Kamarpukur in 1836 A.D. He was named Gadadhar by his parents, which is one of the names of Lord Vishnu. His father, Shree Kshudiram Chattopadhyaya was a very religious man, who spent a lot of time in the worship of the Lord and in the company of Saints. Gadadhar's parents would often tell him stories of great men and Saints. Although he was very intelligent, he was not interested in studies. He would go into deep trance whenever his religious feelings were aroused.

One day when Gadadhar was walking through the fields, he saw a flock of white cranes flying across the dark clouds. So beautiful was the scene that Gadadhar's mind got absorbed in ecstasy. A few hours later, people found him lying in the fields, and got worried. When they woke him up, he pacified everyone, saying that he had entered samadhi, or a trance, by watching the beautiful scene.

When Gadadhar was eight years old, his father passed away. At the age of seventeen, Gadadhar was sent to Calcutta to help his brother, Ramkumar manage his Sanskrit school. Ramkumar wanted Gadadhar to continue his studies in Calcutta, but Gadadhar was more interested in realizing the Highest Truth.

TURNING POINT

Around the same time, Rani Rashmani, a wealthy lady, was establishing a temple of Goddess Kali near Calcutta, along with her son-in-law, Mathur. She was very impressed with Gadadhar and she offered him the position of temple priest. Gadadhar gladly accepted this offer. Mathur changed Gadadhar's name to Ramakrishna.

Ramakrishna loved his new job and performed his duties with great love and devotion. Gradually, this love for the Lord turned into a strong desire to see Him. He prayed day and night and cried bitterly, yearning for the vision of Mother Kali. He would not sleep for many nights at a stretch, and would remain in deep meditation. Finally, he had a vision of the Divine Mother. During this experience, he went into deep samadhi.

Some people understood him to be a great lover of God, while others thought him to have an unstable mind. When his family found out, they decided to get him married in order to divert his attention to worldly affairs, away from his spiritual practices. Ramakrishna was married to Sharada Devi, who later became known as the Holy Mother. Their

marriage remained on a very spiritual plane. Sharada Devi became a strong follower of his teachings, and Ramakrishna worshipped her as a manifestation of the Divine Mother.

SPIRITUAL TRAINING

One day, a religious woman called Bhairavi Brahmani arrived at their house. She told Ramakrishna that she had been sent by Mother Kali to guide him in some spiritual techniques. Through her teachings, Ramakrishna learned yogic techniques and had a Divine vision of God again.

He then began to do devotion in the attitude of Hanuman, or dasya bhav, thinking of himself as the servant of Lord Ram. At the end of this practice, he had a vision of Mother Seeta. Then he did in devotion in the attitude of the gopies, or madhurya bhav, towards Lord Krishna. Such was his absorption in the devotional sentiments of the gopies that he started developing feminine features on his body.

Not much later, a tall yogi called Totapuri came to their house. He had realized God in his formless aspect. Totapuri asked Ramakrishna to meditate on the formless aspect of God. In the beginning, Ramakrishna found it very difficult, because every time he tried, the blissful form of the Divine Mother appeared in his mind. Finally, his mind managed to merge with the formless God. Ramakrishna also studied Islamic and Christian philosophies in order to widen his horizon.

HIS TEACHINGS

Ramakrishna declared that all religions were pointing towards the same God. He gave the example of several ghats (bathing steps) on a lake, belonging to different communities. The Hindus called the water "Jal," the Muslims called it "Pani," and the Christians called it "Water." He said that all three meant the same thing, although the names were different. Similarly, some addressed God as "Brahman," some called him "Christ," while others called him "Ram." However, these were just different names of the same God.

Ramakrishna would say, "Just like you cannot see your face clearly in a dirty mirror; it is difficult to experience Divine Love until the heart is pure. Once the heart is clean, then you can see God by His grace."

HIS FOLLOWING

People thronged to Ramakrishna for spiritual guidance. Everyone who came to him felt spiritually elevated in his association. They started calling him "Paramhansa," or one who, having attained God, is detached from the world. True to his name, Ramakrishna had no desire for anything material. He had known God through various religious paths. He wanted to teach those who had a strong desire to know more about God.

People flocked to him. Finally, one day a young man, Narendranath Dutta came to him. With skepticism, he asked Ramakrishna if he had seen God. Ramakrishna replied, "Yes, I have seen God. I talk to Him and see Him just as I see you now." Narendra was so impressed with Ramakrishna that he surrendered to him. Ramakrishna was waiting for a true disciple and taught the secrets of God-realization to Narendra, who later became famous around the world as Swami Vivekananda. Ramakrishna chose Narendra to spread his teachings worldwide, and personally trained him for the task. Ramakrishna left a handful of disciples under the tutelage of Swami Vivekananda, along with the responsibility of spreading the Divine message across the world.

MAHA SAMADHI

In 1886 A.D., Ramakrishna passed away due to throat cancer. He was 50 years old at that time. Even those who attain the Highest cannot escape death. However, by accepting death so gracefully, Ramakrishna showed that a Saint accepts it too as God's Prasad, or Grace.

|| SWAMI VIVEKANANDA ||

Swami Vivekananda was probably the first Indian Saint to take the Divine knowledge of the Indian scriptures to the Western world. He was the chief disciple of Ramakrishna Paramahansa. Both the Guru and disciple played a major role in the revitalization of Hinduism in modern times.

EARLY YEARS

Swami Vivekananda was born in Kolkata in 1863 A.D. He was named Narendranath Dutta by his parents, who raised him in a very loving environment. His father was a famous lawyer, while his mother was a very religious woman. As a young boy, he was very bright. He was good at sports, studies and music. He enjoyed reading and he showed remarkable power of understanding and retention. As a young man, he had a very curious mind and wondered often about the world and its Creator. He spoke with many scholars about God, but none could satisfy his curiosity.

TURNING POINT

One day, he came across Shree Ramakrishna, a great Saint, who was also known as Swamiji. The first question that Narendra asked Swamiji was, "Have you seen God?" Swamiji smiled and said, "Yes, I have seen God. I talk to Him and see Him just as I see you now. Not only that, I can even show Him to you, if you so desire." Narendra felt that his search had come to an end and that he had finally found his Guru. Shree Ramakrishna too felt like he had found a competent disciple.

For the next five years, Narendra often met Swamiji and learned spiritual secrets from him. During the course of his training under Ramakrishna, Narendra was transformed from a restless, puzzled and impatient youth, to a mature man who was ready to renounce everything for the sake of God-realization. In time, Narendra accepted Ramakrishna as his guru, and surrendered completely with all his heart.

When Ramakrishna left his mortal body, Narendra took charge of organizing his mission and disciples. He encouraged them all to enter the renounced order of sanyas, and wear the saffron robes. The disciples established a Matha, or ashram, for their spiritual practice. Narendranath Dutta now became Swami Vivekananda.

HIS CONTRIBUTIONS

Swami Vivekananda dedicated the rest of his life to the mission. He traveled across India, to better understand the country and its people. When he reached Kanyakumari in Southern India, he reflected on his travels and he realized that the great land of India had gone into stupor due to nine hundred years of foreign rule. It needed to be awakened to its great and glorious past. However, he felt that if India's message was appreciated in the West, it would be more easily accepted in India as well. He decided to go to the West. He also got a vision in which Shree

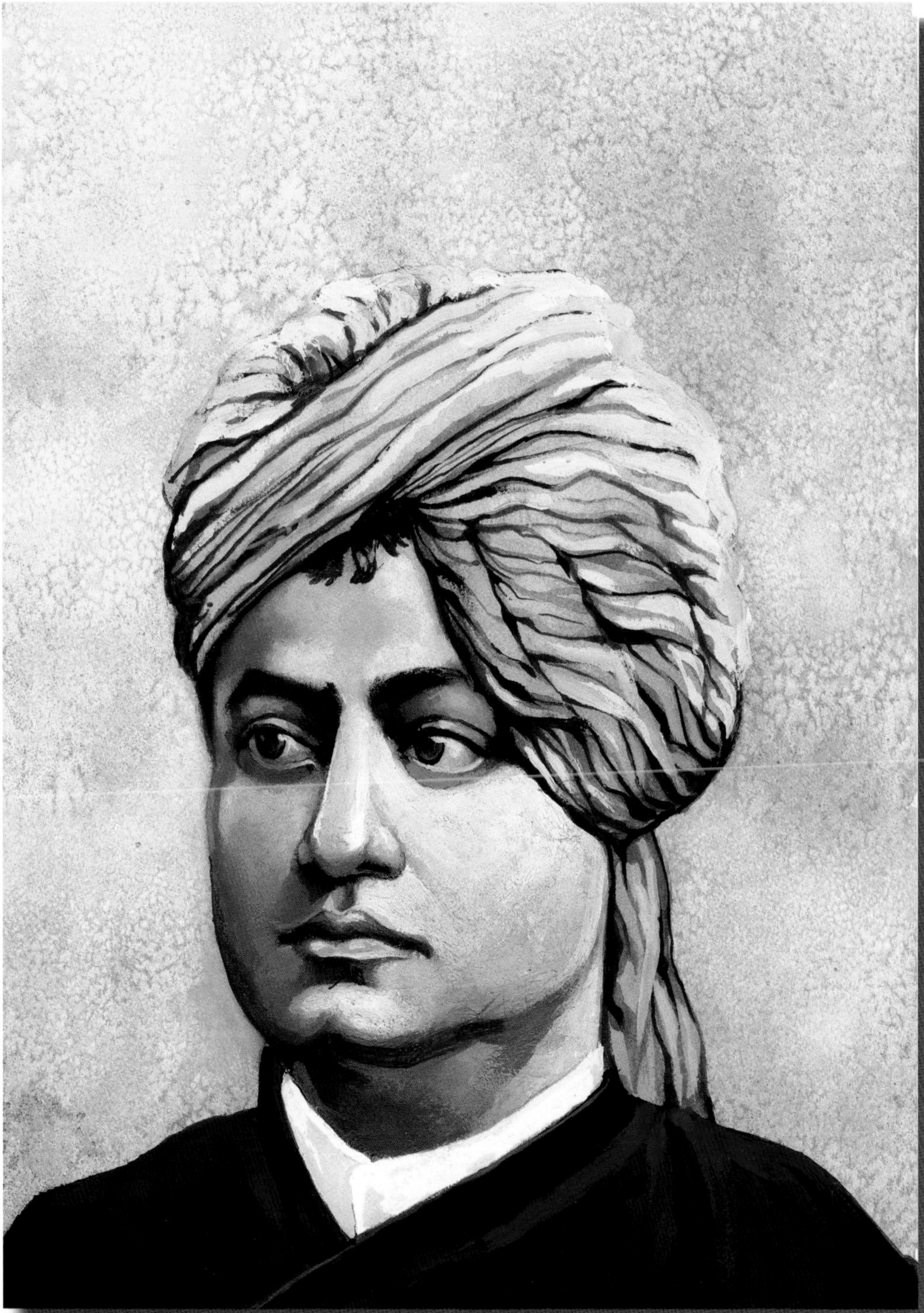

Ramakrishna blessed him for success on his future journey. He then wrote to the holy Mother, Sharada Devi to seek her blessings. Sharada Devi felt that this was God's decision and gave her blessings too.

Swami Vivekananda heard about the Parliament of Religions that was scheduled to be held in Chicago in 1893 A.D. He decided to attend the Parliament, as his first step in his task, to take the message to the West. He sailed to America to attend the Parliament. After reaching Chicago, he realized that he had to be sponsored by an association, in order to attend the Parliament. He did not know anyone in the country and he had very little money. Fortunately, he came across a friendly lady called Kate Sanbom on a train to Boston. Kate invited Swami Vivekananda to stay at her home. There, Swami Vivekananda met one of her friends, Professor Wright. When Professor Wright heard of Swami Vivekananda's problem, he said, "Swamiji, asking you for credentials is like asking the Sun about its right to shine." He wrote a letter to the selection committee of the Parliament of Religions, recommending that they accept Swami Vivekananda. The committee accepted and Swami Vivekananda left for Chicago.

Unfortunately, as luck would have it, Swami Vivekananda lost all his papers, money and the address of the Parliament. As he wandered the streets of Chicago, nobody was willing to help him. He spent the night in an empty wagon in a railroad freight yard. He was woken next morning by a policeman who chased him away. He knocked at the doors of many houses and he was insulted by almost everyone he approached. Luckily, an elderly lady, Mrs. Hale, took pity on his plight and offered him a meal. After the meal, she took him to the Parliament office in her carriage. Finally, Swami Vivekananda had arrived at the Parliament.

When it was his turn to speak to the attendees at the Parliament, he began by addressing his audience as "Sisters and Brothers of America." The audience loved the affectionate and respectful way with which he had addressed them. He won their hearts with his opening line. He then explained to them the meaning of God according to Hinduism. His explanation was very simple as he spoke about the message of universal love. The audience appreciated the message very much.

After the Parliament, he stayed in America for many months giving talks on his message from the Hindu philosophy. The Americans started getting very interested in learning more about India and its traditions. He began the Vedanta Society in New York, and put Swami Sharanananda in charge. After America, Swami Vivekananda went to Europe, where he gave many lectures, as he had done in America. In Europe too, the people loved his talks and they too wanted to learn more about India and its traditions.

Swami Vivekananda finally returned to India in 1897 A.D. By now, people across the country had heard so much about his lectures in America and Europe that they were waiting for his triumphant return to his motherland. He made them all feel proud of the great heritage of India. He inspired his followers to dedicate themselves to God-realization and the service of humanity.

Swami Vivekananda emphasized the importance of service. He showed great sympathy towards everyone who suffered. He believed that every soul was divine and that every person ought to be respected. His followers organized several projects to help the poor and needy in India. He fought hard against all social discriminations based on social group, race or gender. According to him, all humans were pure spirits and hence shared an essential identity.

LAST DAYS

Swami Vivekananda spent the rest of his life in preaching the message of spirituality and universal goodwill. He is regarded as one of India's foremost nation-builders. He inspired the thinking of several other national and international leaders and philosophers. He attained mahasamadhi in 1902 A.D. and passed away at the young age of 39.

‖ JAGADGURU SHREE KRIPALUJI MAHARAJ ‖

Jagadguru Shree Kripaluji Maharaj is the fifth original Jagadguru in Indian history. He is renowned for his exquisite mastery of the Hindu scriptures. He has written thousands of bhajans that exude Vedic philosophy in general and love for God in particular. He is lovingly called "Maharajji" by his devotees.

EARLY YEARS

Maharajji appeared in this world in 1922, on the full moon night called Sharat Poornima. This was the night, when five thousand years ago, Lord Shree Krishna performed His famous Raas Leela dance with the gopies. Maharajji was born in a small village called Mangarh, near Allahabad in Uttar Pradesh, India. A divinely beautiful ashram called Bhakti Dham, or "The Abode of Devotion," has now been built on this place.

Maharajji's childhood was spent in fun and frolic with friends. Yet, he amazed everyone by displaying his mastery in every subject that was taught in school. His answer papers in examinations would always be perfect, but his teachers would hesitate to give him a perfect score, and would award him 99 marks. His friends would be so impressed by this feat, that they had given him the name "Mr. Ninety Nine." He would often take his young village friends to sit under shady village trees, and engage them in singing loving keertans to God.

At the age of fourteen, he left his village Mangarh to study courses from three Universities, at Kashi, Delhi and Kolkata. In those days in India, students were given the facility to register for courses, and study them at home. Due to his exceptional ability, Maharajji completed eighteen years syllabus in a short span of just two-and-a-half years. He received three degrees – Vyakaran Acharya, Sahityacharya, and Ayurved Acharya.

At the young age of sixteen, he gave up his studies and entered the dense forests of Chitrakoot, where he remained absorbed in intense love of Shri Radha Krishna. During that period, he would rest in caves and eat fruits from the trees of the forest. Often, having no awareness of his body, he would go without eating and drinking for several days at a stretch. His mind would remain immersed in Mahabhav, the highest state of devotion to Lord Shree Krishna. This elevated state of Mahabhav devotion was also manifested by another great Saint, Chaitanya Mahaprabhu, about five hundred years ago.

THE KEERTAN MOVEMENT

Great personalities like Jagadguru Shree Kripaluji Maharaj descend in this world to accomplish a grand mission for the welfare of all humankind. So at the age of twenty-two, Maharajji subdued his natural devotion and emerged from the forest. He embarked on his mission of spreading the message of devotion to God. His method of devotion was simple. He would engage people in singing keertans glorifying the Names, Virtues and Pastimes of God. Shree Maharajji himself composed these keertans. His keertan movement spread far and wide in North India.

HONORED AS JAGADGURU

In January 1957, Maharajji was invited to give a series of lectures to the Kashi Vidvat Parishat. This was a body of 500 foremost Vedic scholars of India, each of whom was a master of one or more scriptures. Maharajji spoke in Sanskrit for ten days, giving innumerable quotations from the Vedas, Puranas, Mahabharat, Ramayan, Vedant, and other scriptures. He showed the wonderful unity in the teachings of the previous Jagadgurus and revealed the true path of God realization.

When the entire body of scholars was convinced that Kripaluji Maharaj's knowledge was deeper than the combined knowledge of all the 500 scholars put together, they honored him with the title of Jagadguru, or the Spiritual Master of the world. Jagadguru in Hinduism is like the Pope in Christianity. There have been four original Jagadgurus in history before Shree Maharajji – Jagadguru Shankaracharya, Jagadguru Nimbarkacharya, Jagadguru Ramanujacharya, Jagadguru Madhvacharya. Jagadguru Shree Kripaluji Maharaj became the fifth original Jagadguru in history. The scholars of Kashi also declared that he was Jagadguruttam, or supreme amongst Jagadgurus, and Bhaktiyog Rasavatar, or the descension of the Bliss of Divine Love.

WORLDWIDE MISSION

Maharajji then traveled extensively in India, delivering discourses unraveling the secrets of the scriptures. People would come to listen to him in tens of thousands, attracted by his charming personality and impressed by his extraordinary knowledge. He made the deepest scriptural truths accessible to everyone in the simplest language. His unique style of blending humor, worldly knowledge and practical examples with the knowledge from the scriptures left a deep mark on all who had the good fortune to listen to him.

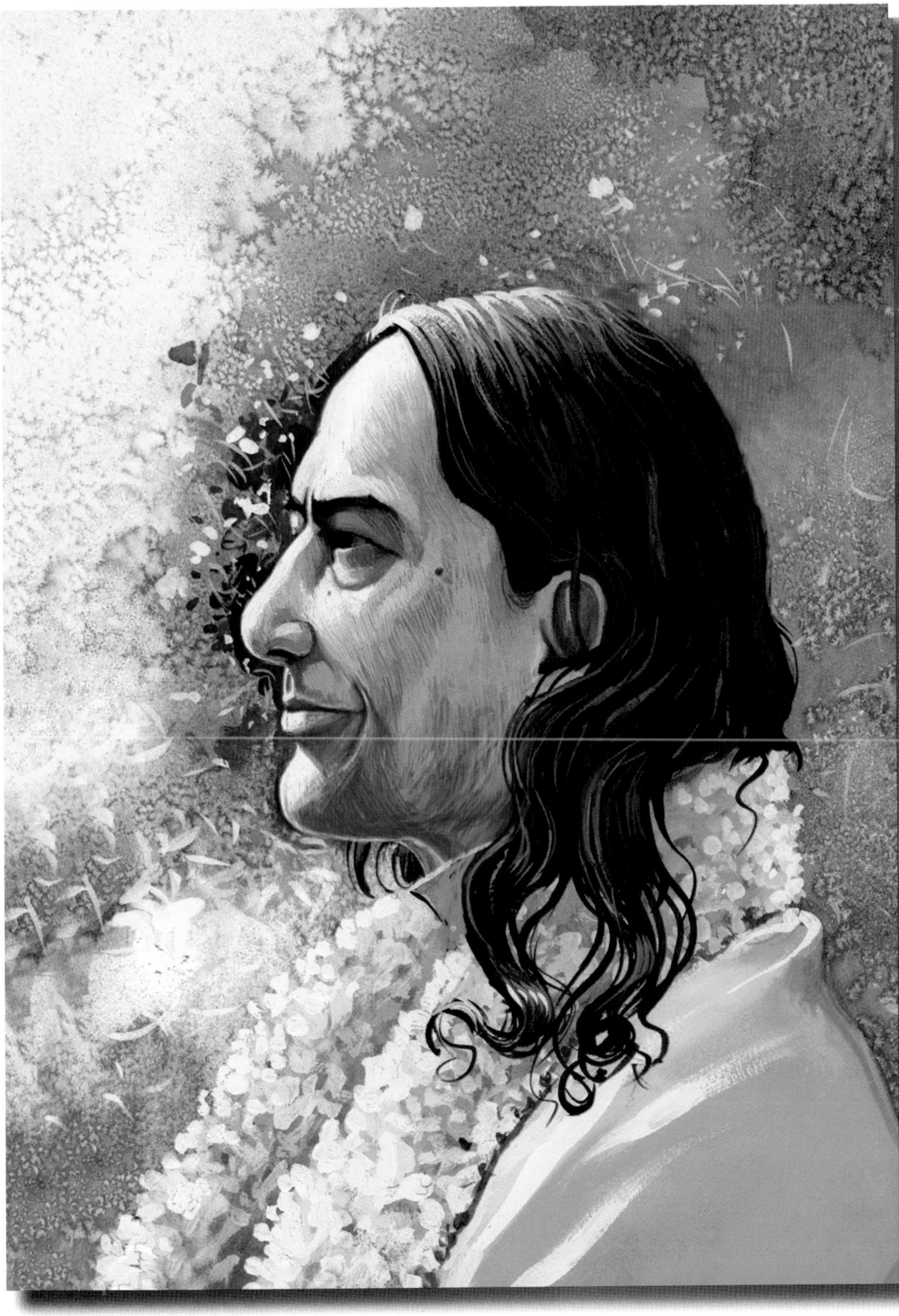

To enable his teachings to spread worldwide, Jagadguru Shree Kripaluji Maharaj began training sanyasi preachers and sending them to different parts of the globe. He also established his mission by constructing huge ashrams to provide facilities for devotees who wished to apply the teachings in their lives practically. Jagadguru Kripalu Yog is a part of this worldwide mission.

Maharajji's Divinity often gets revealed in subtle ways. For example, if his lotus feet are washed, the water, which is called charanamrta, becomes highly sacred. If that water is kept for decades, it does not decay. Devotees often keep his charanamrta in their homes, and sip it from time to time, to experience Maharajji's blessings. After his youth, Maharajji never spent any time reading the scriptures. Yet he is able to quote any verse from any scripture. He thus reveals that he has knowledge of all the verses of all the scriptures. It is as if all the Vedas are open before him when he speaks.

HIS TEACHINGS

Jagadguru Shree Kripaluji Maharaj explains that God is an ocean of Divine Bliss. We souls are His tiny parts, and so it is our nature to seek Bliss or happiness. However, we have forgotten our identity as eternal souls, and we are thinking of ourselves to be the material body. So we are searching for happiness in worldly objects. This can never satisfy the soul. The unlimited happiness we are seeking can only be attained from God, and so we must all make God-realization the goal of our lives.

He also teaches that God is beyond our senses, mind and intellect. We cannot see him with our effort. However, by His Grace He can be seen and attained. To receive the Grace of God, we must engage in devotion to Him.

Maharajji explains that to do bhakti, it is not necessary to leave the world. One can practice karmyog, which means to perform the worldly duties with the body and keep the mind engaged in God. To attain this state of karmyog, we must make some time in our daily schedule,